IMAGES OF WAR

The Germans in Flanders 1915-1916

RARE PHOTOGRAPHS FROM WARTIME ARCHIVES

DAVID BILTON

'Belgium will be our grave.'

Pen & Sword
MILITARY

First published in Great Britain in 2012 by
PEN & SWORD MILITARY
an imprint of
Pen & Sword Books Ltd
47 Church Street
Barnsley
South Yorkshire
S70 2AS

Copyright © David Bilton 2012

ISBN 978 1 84884 878 8

Typeset in Gill Sans

Printed and bound in England by
CPI Group (UK) Ltd, Croydon, CR0 4YY

Pen & Sword Books Ltd incorporates the Imprints of Pen & Sword Aviation, Pen & Sword Family History, Pen & Sword Maritime, Pen & Sword Military, Pen & Sword Discovery, Wharncliffe Local History, Wharncliffe True Crime, Wharncliffe Transport, Pen & Sword Select, Pen & Sword Military Classics, Leo Cooper, The Praetorian Press, Remember When, Seaforth Publishing and Frontline Publishing

For a complete list of Pen & Sword titles please contact
PEN & SWORD BOOKS LIMITED
47 Church Street, Barnsley, South Yorkshire, S70 2AS, England
E-mail: enquiries@pen-and-sword.co.uk
Website: www.pen-and-sword.co.uk

Contents

Acknowledgements

The book turned into three. Sorry to everyone at home, and thanks.

As with previous books, a great big thank you to Anne Coulson for her help in checking the text and to The Prince Consort's Library for all their help.

Errors of omission or commission are mine alone.

Not all barracks were permanent. Here a large marquee to is being erected to house returning troops.

Introduction

The purpose of this series of books, *The Germans in Flanders 1914*, *The Germans in Flanders 1915-1916* and *The Germans in Flanders 1917-1918*, is not to analyse, in any depth, the strategic, tactical, political or economic reasons for the fighting in Flanders but rather to chronicle the events that happened there during 1914 – 1918 and how events elsewhere impacted upon these. The brief words rely on the pictures to tell much of the story: pictures from a private collection and from texts published during the period of this history (detailed in the bibliography). The books are not necessarily a chronological photographic record as some periods were more fully recorded than others and in many cases what was photographed in 1915 was just as valid a record as if it had been taken in 1918; in fact, these books are more an attempt to provide a cameo of the experiences of the German Army in Flanders during the Great War. For most of the time, armies do not fight, and the photographs portray life outside the trenches as well as in them.

As with my earlier books on the German Army, I have included a day-to-day chronology to show what was happening across the Belgian Flanders Front from the German point of view. However, as Flanders is a coastal area and the occupied territory closest to the British mainland, the book also deals with events at sea and information about aerial activity.

Most of the book is centred on Ypres and its immediate environs because that is where the actual fighting occurred. However, most of Belgium was occupied; the effect of the war was sometimes felt directly, more often indirectly, throughout the country.

Flanders also provided the German air force with numerous bases, some of which were used to attack England. 'Quite regularly since 1914, single-engined aeroplanes had braved

The remains of Zonnebeke church.

the Channel, one or two at a time, to drop a few small bombs along the coast. Their favourite target was Dover Harbour.' They had become a routine nuisance.

Zeppelins were usually employed for bombing, but in late 1916 an aircraft from Flanders bombed London. Lieutenant Ilges (photographer and bomb aimer) and Deck Officer Brandt (pilot), both naval airmen, took off from Mariakerke near the Belgian coast in a single-engine LVG biplane; primarily a reconnaissance aircraft, it had the range to take it to London and could be equipped with bombs. Ilges had photographed the coast on many occasions but had not gone far inland. The flight, unlike the previous coastal trips, was a meandering journey through Essex and up the Thames. During the trip Ilges photographed 'aerodromes, factories, docks and other choice targets' and then, above London, he took more pictures before releasing his load of six twenty-pound bombs. Brandt flew south, managing to evade the British squadrons at Dover and Dunkirk, but

Crown Prince Wilhelm, the Kaiser's son, with his entourage, watching training manoeuvres in Flanders.

engine trouble ended the flight over French lines and the two were taken prisoner. Little notice was taken of the flight or the capture of its crew. The British 'were too busy exulting over the two Zeppelins' that had been shot down. However, *The Times* warned in an editorial that it was likely that there would be further such visits on an extended scale. The following summer 'German bombers came to London in formation.'

Flanders was an important area for naval offensive operations and had to be guarded against Entente naval attack and the possibility of naval-supported invasion. To this effect the sea-front was guarded by regiments of marine artillery. 'Thirty guns of the heaviest calibre had been set up there, among them five of 38 cm., four of 30.5 cm., and besides them a large number of quick-firing guns from 10.5 to 21 cm. calibre.' Manning these fortifications and the coastal trenches employed large numbers of men.

The Naval Corps, the troops defending the naval areas, was instituted under the leadership of Admiral von Schröder on September 3, 1914, and played a part in the taking of Antwerp on October 10, 1914. *Naval Corps General Command* had its headquarters at Bruges. Its infantry consisted of three regiments of able seamen and the marines. The latter in particular played a part in the great battles in Flanders in 1916 and 1917.

Again, taking the offensive to the Royal Navy required boats, aircraft and of course submarines. In 1916, a quarter of all available U-boats were assigned to the *Naval Corps* in Flanders. Initially they were small, relatively slow boats but later models were over three times the weight and half as fast again. However, their limited range meant that they could operate from Flanders only against the south and east coasts of England. Most mine-laying submarines also operated from the Flanders coast. Zeebrugge was an important base for the maintenance of these submarine types. 'When the U-boat campaign opened on February 1, 1917, there were already 57 boats in the North Sea' of which 'the Naval Corps in Flanders had at its disposal 31 U-boats of different types.'

A war remembrance card showing the surroundings of Kemmel near Ypres.

While Flanders was a strategically important area, not every day is listed; as on every other front during the war, some days were very active but most were no more or less significant than the previous one. For a missing day the GHQ report simply read: 'In Flanders today again only artillery activity' or 'In the West nothing new' – in English, the famous words: 'All quiet on the Western Front'.

The reality underlying the fact of this bland statement is revealed in the letters home of Lothar Dietz, a Philosophy student

A charity card sent by a soldier in *I Landwehr Division*, showing one method of moving heavy howitzers through the Flanders mud.

from Leipzig, who was killed near Ypres on 15 April 1915. 'You at home can't have the faintest idea of what it means to us when in the newspaper it simply and blandly says: "In Flanders to-day again only artillery activity". Far better to go over the top in the most foolhardy attack, cost what it may, than stick it out all day long under shell-fire, wondering all the time whether the next one will maim one or blow one to bits'.

'Flanders is the ancient name for the mostly flat countryside that stretches from the North Sea coast in Belgium south to the French coast along the English Channel.' Its name in Flemish means "flooded land". In the present day its size is classed as roughly equivalent to Greater Los Angeles. Its average temperature is around nine degrees Celsius and it rains practically every other day. However, the centuries-old drainage system amply coped with the excess of water, creating a fertile land where farmers produced crops of 'beets, turnips and potatoes as well as flax, cotton, tobacco, grain, and fodder. They kept cattle, sheep, and pigs, chickens, geese, and ducks.'

Flanders is very difficult to define geographically; it has been in a continuous state of flux for hundreds of years. Originally covering a much larger area than today, what was Flanders during the war differed according to the army in which a soldier fought. To the Belgian army it was a defined area that covered the unconquered part of their nation and part of the conquered territory; to the French it was the area of Belgium that they were fighting in; to the British it covered their Front from just north of Arras in France to their furthest left boundary at Boesinghe, north of Ypres. For the German Army, the Flanders Front stretched from Dixmude in the north to Frelinghien in the south, opposite the area held by the French and the British, but, to the General Staff at *OHL*, Flanders also included the conquered coastal regions of Belgium and their defenders, the *Kaiserliche Marine*, sea soldiers who guarded the coast and fought in the trenches. As this book is about the German Army, it is their geographical understanding of Flanders (Flandern) that has been used; activity in French Flanders is only mentioned in passing where it relates to the events in Belgium.

The area from the Belgian coast down to Arras witnessed some of the most intense and fierce fighting of the war, fighting equalled only by that at Verdun and on the Somme

— battles that occurred during the period covered by this book — a period which was, nevertheless, one of relative quiet for the Flanders Front.

The channel ports were a strategic German objective at the beginning of the war and the Allies needed to keep the ports open for the BEF; Flanders was clearly an area that would be fought over until one side won. A German success would enable their armies to strike at Britain and press southwards in an encircling movement against Paris.

Belgian Flanders lies at or just above sea level. This fact, coupled with the poor drainage caused by continuous shelling, meant that this war was often fought in a sea of mud. The flat ground made any eminence, even one as low as thirty feet, take on a tactical importance for both sides; holding the high ground gave the defender a view of his enemy. Holding 'a hill of 150 feet was priceless for the observation and artillery control that it provided over enemy lines and their gun positions'.

Ypres lies in a basin formed by a maritime plain intersected by canals, and dominated on the north, north-east and south by low wooded hills. The canals, the Yser being the most important, follow a south-east to north-east direction; a number of streams flow in the same direction and there are three large ponds: Dickebusch, Zillebeke and Bellewaarde.

The hills that form the sides of the Ypres basin are very low and, at that time, were partly wooded. Their crests run through Houthulst Forest, Poelcapelle, Passchendaele, Broodseinde, Becelaere, Gheluvelt, Hill 60 and St. Eloi. Further south is the Messines-Wytschaete ridge, and to the south-west are the Hills of Flanders.

Houthulst Forest was the largest of the woods. Further south, after Westroosebeke, Passchendaele and Zonnebeke were other woods that were to become famous: Polygone, Nonne-Bosschen (Nonnes), Glencorse, Inverness and Herentage.

Surrounded by low hills, the numerous small waterways and the area's maritime climate gave the area around Ypres a character that was different to the rest of the front. The marshy ground, almost at sea level, is 'further sodden by constant rain and mists', forming a spongy mass that made it impossible to dig trenches or underground shelters. The water level is very near the surface, making parapets the only suitable and possible type of defence-works. Shell craters immediately filled with water and became death traps for

A card sent in early October 1915 by Unteroffizier Kollusayer of *12 Bavarian Reserve Infantry Regiment* in *1 Bavarian Reserve Division* to Munich. Stationed on the Arras front and serving in a unit that had not served in Belgium, he sent home a photograph of troops warming themselves around a fire near Dixmude.

The grisly remains of an airman shot down over Flanders.

the wounded, careless or unlucky. Such images create the iconography of the Flanders battles.

The geology and geography of the area meant that both sides centred their defence 'around the woods, villages and numerous farms, which were converted into redoubts with concrete blockhouses and deep wire entanglements'. Any slight piece of higher ground was fiercely contested. The dominating hill crests 'were used as observation posts – the lowering sky being usually unfavourable for aerial observation – while their counter-slopes masked the concentrations of troops for the attacks.' As a result the fighting was at its most intense along the crests and around the fortified farms.

Throughout the area 'were numerous scattered villages, clumps of woodland, a few nineteenth-century chateaux and occasional farms with thick hedges marking the bound-aries of their largely open fields. On slightly rising ground in the centre' of the area was 'a slumbering town with Gothic spires and towers'.

In the Middle Ages, Ypres had been a populous town of some 40,000. During this time it was the centre of the Flemish wool trade and was famous across Europe for its cloth fair. 'At Nieuport ships from England and the   se Baltic ports entered the river, making their way upstream to the centre of the town, some unloading their cargoes at a covered quay within the Cloth Hall itself.'

Having survived plague, pestilence and the migration of many weavers to healthier towns, the town was attacked by the French and then the English. For three centuries, war swept western Flanders with weary regularity. Even in Tudor times the Belgian lands were already dubbed "the cockpit of Europe". Ypres was frequently besieged. After centuries of fighting by the French, Dutch and Spanish, the peace treaty after the fall of Napoleon allowed West Flanders and eight other Belgian provinces to be incorporated into the United Kingdom of the Netherlands. In 1830, an independent Belgium was created, whose neutrality was guaranteed nine years later by the Treaty of London.

By 1914 Ypres numbered under 17,000 occupants. Its commerce was based around the manufacture of flax, lace, ribbons, cotton and soap. It was a minor tourist area because of its medieval Cloth Hall, the largest non-religious Gothic building in Europe. The newly

The interior of St. Vaast church in Menin. The card was sent by a soldier in the *Guards Corps*.

22. — Menin· Intérieur de l'Eglise St-

arrived British troops found it to be 'a gem of a town with its lovely old-world gabled houses, red-tiled roofs, and no factories visible to spoil the charm.'

The *OHL* history described why the area was so heavily contested. The possession of Ypres to the English was a point of honour. For both sides it was the central pivot of operations. From the time artillery fire could reach the town, it became a legitimate target for German gunners because it lay so close to the front that the German advance could be seen from its towers — so claimed the *OHL* history of the battle. It also concealed enemy batteries and sheltered their reserves. Captain Schwink wrote in 1917 that 'for

The butcher's shop before and after a bombardment clearly showing the damage to the eighteenth century front.

120913-1

Visé Paris N° 10315-150

the sake of our troops we had to bring it under fire; for German life is more precious than the finest Gothic architecture.'

At the start of the war Ypres did not even appear on newspaper maps. By 1916, it not only appeared in newspapers but had become a sacred place, like the Somme and Verdun. During the period covered by this book, the town was in ruins.

The Ypres salient was key to the fighting on the front which can be divided into three major battles known to the British as First, Second and Third Ypres, but there were many smaller battles between the major offensives and a final offensive – not centred around Ypres – through Belgium that by the German Army, followed by the final Allied attack to liberate Belgium. The first battle was a result of a powerful German offensive – a counter-stroke to the battles of the Yser – then an attempt to take Ypres; during this battle arose the myth of the students valiantly storming the British defences. 'The second stage was marked by British and Franco-British offensives, begun in the second half of 1916 and considerably developed during the summer and autumn of the following year.'

It was essentially a British sector with Belgian and French troops at the northern end and, in September 1918, two American divisions were engaged. Most of the towns and villages were fought over again and again, for each was key to the next piece. Casualties were consistently high and artillery barrages long, ferocious and expensive. By 1917 little remained of the 1914 landscape. A fertile land had by then become a moonscape.

When Belgium rejected the German ultimatum to allow free passage of troops through the country to invade France, Belgium was brought into the European War. By 1916, after fourteen months of heavy fighting, both sides were entrenched close to their original positions. Centre stage would now move to Verdun and then the Somme.

Of the hundreds of thousands of men who served in Flanders, two are notable – Winston Churchill and Adolf Hitler. As a volunteer, Hitler served throughout the war with *16 Bavarian Reserve Infantry Regiment,* in *6 Bavarian Reserve Division.* After being involved in the 1914 Ypres battles, the division was never again used in a lead assault role, becoming a static front-holding division, good in defence. Churchill's stay in trenches was

A photograph taken on 27 January 1915 of staff officers in Lüttich. Each officer has signed the reverse and given their town of residence before the war. The card was posted at the German postal facilities in the main railway station at Lüttich on 8 February to Hannover.

A before and after comparison of the photographer's own shop. Antony was the premier Ypres photographer who in numerous postcards pictorially chronicled the destruction of the town.

more limited. On 24 January, 6 Royal Scots Fusiliers, recovering from heavy losses at Loos, went into the line at Ploegsteert with Churchill as their commanding officer. After 100 days of sharing their privations, helped by supplies of brandy and port and a limber containing a bath – and a boiler to heat the bath water – he returned to his political activities in London a few weeks before his battalion, merged with 7 Royal Scots Fusiliers, went over the top on the Somme.

The Flanders front was never as quiet a front as some other parts – for instance the southern sector of the Vosges – of the Western Front were. But at times of relative inactivity it was used by both sides as a rest area. In Flanders 'the Germans had a rest-house for their troops along the Yser in the woods of Praetbos, near Esen and Vladso.' It was a quiet spot to raise spirits, where the men could play football and watch films.

Throughout 1916, Verdun and the Somme were the main battle zones so Flanders was used as an area in which to rest, recuperate and refit before returning to the war. The post-war Michelin guide to the Flanders battlefields describes the period covered by this book as a period of comparative calm, interrupted by Second Ypres and followed by a long period of comparative calm with isolated actions and artillery activity on both sides.

'The first fortnight of 1915 was comparatively quiet. During the second fortnight a strong German attack broke down before the front-line trenches near Bixschoote. The continual rains in this previously flooded district rendered all activity impossible, save that of the artillery, which continued to bombard unceasingly during February. It was only the first half of March that the opposing armies became really active.' In Flanders the activity was by the German Army; the British were too heavily involved at Neuve-Chapelle. With improving weather, the number of local engagements increased and the bombardment continued. Local attacks gave way to a powerful attempt to take Ypres during which poison gas was used.

June was quiet as the focus turned on the Argonne, Artois and Champagne. 'Nevertheless, local actions took place from time to time without any appreciable result.' This comparative calm included mining operations, gas attacks and severe bombardments of the front-line and Ypres.

The year finished with the first phosgene attack on the Western Front. On the night of 4/5 December, a non-commissioned officer of *XXVI. Reserve Corps* was captured near Ypres. He told his British captors about the gas cylinders along the corps front, and that there was to have been an attack but it had been postponed. Information from another source indicated the likelihood of an attack somewhere in Flanders after 10 December when the weather was suitable. At the same time *26 (Württemberg) Division* arrived from the Eastern Front.

At 0500 hours on 19 December, in the dark, an unusual type of single parachute flare lit the sky followed fifteen minutes later by red rockets along the whole *XXVI. Reserve Corps* front. Shortly afterwards the gas was released and the German front line opened fire. A British shrapnel barrage discouraged an attack but isolated groups attempted to get to the British lines. The Germans then put down an intense bombardment northwest of Wieltje. About 0615 hours green rockets heralded the commencement of a gas shell barrage, followed by heavy howitzer fire. With daylight the Germans were able to put up an observation balloon and send reconnaissance aircraft up. No attack followed.

The calm continued into 1916 with attempts to cross the Yser during February and an assault on The Bluff. Created by the spoil from failed attempts to dig a canal, its height on a relatively flat landscape made it an important military objective. German forces took The Bluff in February 1916, and it was recaptured by the British on 2 March.

Even though von Falkenhayn had passed over Flanders as an area for future offensives on account of the state of the ground, in April the fighting intensified with attacks near St. Eloi and along the Ypres-

OORLOG 1914-1915
Ruinen te Poperinghe — Ruines de Poperinghe
Ruins of Poperinghe
Sᵗ-Bertens kerk beschadigd door een obus
Eglise Sᵗ-Bertin

Shell damage to the houses near St. Berten's Church in Poperinghe.

A photograph taken in Ypres. On the left is a Red Cross worker Geoffrey Young, in the centre the Burgomaster of Ypres, Rene Colaert, and on the right Count Delauny of the Belgian medical services, attached to the French Army.

Langemarck road, the prelude to assaults further south near Armentières. These attacks gained little, and ceased at the end of June.

'In July 1916, the Germans detonated a mine under the ridge, but did not capture it. The Germans took The Bluff during the Spring Offensive of 1918, and it finally returned to Allied hands on 28 September after a push by the 14th (Light) Division', the division that had recaptured it in March 1916. 'From July, 1916, to May, 1917, the Ypres sector remained comparatively quiet. There were few attacks on either side, but the guns thundered day and night.'

'During 1916, the German Army lost 434,000 men between 21 February and 18 December during its attempt to destroy the French army at Verdun, and a further 500,000 while countering the Franco-British attack at the Somme in July. Although the French lost more than 500,000 at Verdun and the British and French together sustained another 600,000 casualties on the Somme, the front-line positions remained largely unchanged.' On 29 September Falkenhayn was replaced.

During the battles of 1915 and 1916 a new form of offensive warfare developed in the German Army. The new assault detachments or Stosstruppen, based on the raiding parties of the first two years of the war, were tasked with taking the war into the enemy's trenches. By 1918 these units were the elite of the army.

Throughout the book German units are identified by italics and British and French troops by standard lettering.

Chapter One

1915 – The Spring Offensive

Drinking the New Year in, the toast was 'a wish for us all for 1915: may this new year make up for 1914 and bring us peace'. There was no firing and for a few hours they were able to forget the present in France. In Flanders the artillery duels started almost immediately.

A 1915 postcard showing the fires caused during the shelling of the Cloth Hall on 22 November 1914.

On lookout in the trenches, viewing the enemy trenches through a slit in bullet-proof plate placed between the sandbags.

Unlike its enemies, Germany was the only combatant fighting a war on two fronts. 'At the beginning of 1915, the war in the east was not going well for Germany or Austria-Hungary.' Despite victories at Tannenburg and the Masurian lakes, the situation was far from stable. In the south, Austro-Hungarian forces had failed to defeat the smaller Serbian Army, Russian forces pressed deep into Austrian Galicia and by the end of the year had inflicted over a million casualties on the Austro-Hungarian forces. 'Austria-Hungary was threatened with collapse.'

'In the West, Germany's offensives had also failed to secure a victory, but there the front was stabilising, with trench warfare becoming the norm from Belfort near the Swiss border to Nieuport on the English Channel. Falkenhayn's attempts to capture the Channel Ports and then the city of Ypres with a late-autumn Flanders offensive resulted only in disappointment and heavy casualties.' Faced with a struggling ally, a difficult political situation in the Balkans and a war on two fronts, the future did not look as bright for Germany as it had in August 1914. However, on both sides of the conflict, the protagonists had problems, and on both sides, they each looked to victory.

The start of 1915 saw leaders on both sides, even though they did not yet possess the manpower, ability or tactics to achieve it, aiming at victory through the use of more and more heavy artillery and longer barrages. Just enough pressure would buckle the opponent's ability to defend and troops would rush through to ensure a quick victory. Both sides prepared their plans; but the year would prove to bring the French their highest casualty rate of the war and little gain to any of the combatant nations on the Western Front.

January saw considerable activity on the Western Front, particularly from the French who launched attacks in the Champagne, Somme, Argonne, Alsace and Artois, with successes and losses on both sides. During this time the Flanders front was never at rest; of the four attacks along this front during January, three were by the Entente, none gained anything of importance. However, they did inflict casualties.

There were also numerous small raids and it was not always the British who were on the defensive. At around 2000 hours on 3 January, one British officer with twenty-five men crossed the 200 yards of no man's land. Their target was a short trench occupied by officers and around thirty men that had been dug outwards from a sap head, all being guarded by two sentries. Unfortunately there was no was no wire in place so the attackers had easy access. The attackers crept noiselessly to the trench and managed to bayonet the sentries. 'All the occupants were asleep and were bayoneted; the officer's head was broken in with the butt end of a rifle – not a shot was fired – some men set to work at once, and cut the ground from the adjacent ditch thus flooding the trench.' The whole attack lasted fifteen minutes.

The Ypres salient was the responsibility of *Fourth Army,* commanded by Duke Albrecht von Württemberg. As the front included coastal areas, the conflict on the Flanders front involved naval action and, as in every other sector, aerial combat was in the ascendant. 'The towns from Westende to Zeebrugge on the North Sea coast remained the focus of daily firefights and minor operations. Enemy warships of all kinds – including submarines and torpedo boats – often appeared off the coast while aircraft bombed the occupied towns and fortifications. German airforce squadrons and the coastal batteries of the Naval Corps conducted the defence without difficulty. The Germans also launched remote operations against the enemy's interior: bomber squadrons attacked the staging areas of Dunkirk a number of times, while German aircraft patrolled the sea all the way to the British coast. Around the same time, German submarine activity out of Zeebrugge began.'

Allied propaganda portrayed the German soldier as a vandal and barbarian. Every army has its share of scoundrels. Most are not like this. Ludwig Finke was a principled soldier who took care to protect what was sacred.

Towards the end of February he was stationed at Wilskerke between Ostend and Nieuport. He wrote home describing his barracks. 'I am sitting at the High Altar of a beautiful, big, village church. In a choir-stall lie the remains of my evening meal. My writing-desk is the altar, at the foot of which I lie, rolled up in my blanket on a heap of straw, and sleep dreamlessly as we travel-worn soldiers do sleep – as long as we can. Up here in my corner I don't allow any coarse, army jokes. If we are compelled to use the churches, we can at least behave decently in them. All the valuable things that were lying about, and which I have learned from childhood to honour and regard as sacred, I carefully preserved, folded and laid together, and asked the Battalion-Commander to keep an eye on them. We don't want to be vandals'.

When the army invaded Belgium, there were many reprisals against towns where it was thought that civilians had shot at German soldiers. This fear of franc-tireurs and spies continued throughout the war. To reduce the risk of sabotage and subterfuge a curfew existed. In Wilskerke, within the range of enemy guns, half the inhabitants were 'boxed up, as being under suspicion, from 6 o'clock in the evening, under guard.'

Garrison troops in the main street of Westroosbecke. The postcard was sent by Wehrmann August Raphael to his girlfriend in Lüneburg in May 1915. Raphael was serving as an gunner in 2 Battery of a Landwehr Field artillery unit that was part of a mobile ersatz unit.

While many had fled, those that had stayed behind worked for the occupying forces. Many coastal towns were holiday resorts so many of their hotels were shut up but Ostend managed to remain a relatively vibrant town because it was some distance behind the lines and because of the soldiers in the area: 'Field-Grey troops from the Front, blue Landsturm, sailors in their becoming uniform', they 'crowd the streets, look in at the shop-windows, stroll on the boulevards and fill the restaurants and cafés which have all donned as it were a little German cloak in order to have the attraction of being "home-like"'.

It was to be over four months into the year before a big attack in the Ypres area was launched, but in the meantime there were smaller operations by both sides. In the first few weeks nothing of real importance occurred: an attack by *53 Saxon Reserve Division* in the sector southwest of Passchendaele was partially successful and an attack by a Moroccan unit successfully repulsed.

The two principal attacks were in French Flanders and at St. Eloi, south of Ypres in Belgian Flanders; the latter was against unseasoned British troops and lasted for a number of days. A month later, on 14 March, after two mines and a surprise late afternoon attack, the British 28 Division fell back, allowing the attacking troops to capture St. Eloi village, the trenches near it, and the 'Mound' (a half acre, thirty foot high artificial mound of earth) to the south of the village. The next day, all the gains were lost to a British counter-attack, except the 'Mound' which provided good observation over British positions.

After the offensive at Neuve Chapelle, the British bowed to the French request to release two of their corps from the Ypres Salient by extending their line as far as the Ypres-Poelcapelle road, with sixteen British divisions facing eleven and a half defending divisions. In some of the areas taken over from the French lay the bodies of French and German troops who had been killed during the 1914 Ypres battles. In such positions, mostly on the Gravenstafel Ridge towards Passchendaele and Poelcapelle, the acrid smell of death was in the air; it was so strong that even chloride of lime could not expunge it.

Both sides relied upon belts of wire for defence, and nowhere could the soldier dig far below the surface because of the high water table. Troops resided in shallow holes in the

near Nieuport.

French troops in the front line near Nieuport. Note the wooden fire step.

ground under roofs of corrugated iron, logs or timber; these were more splinter-proof than shell-proof.

The departure of the French, and their anti-aircraft guns, gave the air force a greater freedom to assist artillery registration on British positions and increased the number of bombing missions on Ypres and the surrounding villages. The army, on the other hand, sent out few patrols to harass the newly in-position British troops, preferring to increase their defences. Across no man's land opposite the British trenches, the wire entanglements grew every night and every morning the parapets were thicker. Even though the British positions were clearly inferior, they were left alone, allowing their generals to look to the future and a joint offensive.

After the failure of the Entente forces to break through German positions, *OHL* realised that their defensive preparations had been sufficient to halt any progress of their enemies. This regained confidence, despite smaller troop numbers, caused *OHL* to forgo temporarily their offensive plans on the Western Front in favour of the Galician front. This did not though preclude attacks in the west.

As the two Entente armies planned their offensive, their deliberations were halted abruptly by an attack in the neighbourhood of Ypres. This importantly influenced the Allied offensive plan by leading to a withdrawal of their troops from the intended battle area and making them use up accumulated reserves of materiel and ammunition.

On 14 April at 1115 hours, after four days' artillery activity, a mine exploded under the British positions at St.Eloi to the south of Ypres, followed by a methodical bombardment of the British positions. There was a counter barrage by British artillery, but no infantry attacked. An attack using asphyxiating gas was planned for two days later, but was postponed to wait for better conditions.

While the commanding officers planned their next assault, Private Finke wrote home about his expeditions upon the dunes near Westende. 'I much enjoy my expeditions among the dunes. Armed with a walking-stick I set off, always straight ahead till I reach the dunes, for in the meadows there is danger of shrapnel'.

The area had been hotly contested months before and everywhere there were traces of the battles. 'The way lies through old positions; there are shell-smashed rifles, empty Belgian haversacks, behind every mound of earth, from which the fellows were chased

Recently captured Belgian officers under armed escort. The Unteroffizier at the front is carrying some of the officers' swords.

by our marine battalions. Here and there, among the heather and scrub, a lonely grave, the weather-beaten wooden cross adorned by a marine-helmet or a bullet-perforated sailor's cap'.

Deserted buildings dotted the area: 'every now and then a peasant's dwelling in the midst of its well-tilled patch of ground, the house a ruin, empty, with ragged scraps of clothing, broken crockery and rubbish in the living-room, and the cellars still full of potatoes. The cupboards torn open, pictures and photographs blowing about in the breeze.'

One particular house, the Villa Scolaire, epitomised the severity of the fighting. 'The fighting just at this spot must have been terrific, both on the French and German side. Shell-holes and fragments of metal, rifles, dud shells and fuses, helmets and képis, knapsacks and belts. But also many graves, which the marines have adorned according to their own taste with patterns of shell-cases and duds, flowers and bits of glass, arabesques of shrapnel bullets between or bits of stuff and ornaments'.

There were never enough billets for the occupying troops. When the line had settled down it was possible to start the construction of purpose built huts. Here a poineer unit is building a new encampment

Being stationed near the sea could provide resting troops with a respite from the war and a chance to dream. Just over two weeks before his death at Nieuport, Ludwig Finke described what it felt like on the dunes. 'There foamy crests of the steel-blue billows roll to one's feet; the cloudless spring sky stretches above the wide sheet of water; the waves splash and prattle; the shifting sand sings and hums; the sun shines in the midday splendour over the silent and solitary dunes. And the stormy-petrel shoots up into the air above the white, softly undulating crests, and away out into the distance over the sea. If one could but fly with him!'

On the morning of 21 April, Falkenhayn held a conference with the commanding officer of *Fourth Army* insisting on an early execution of the gas attack. Falkenhayn told the Duke of Württemberg that his army 'should not aim for too wide an objective, but rather execute the attack at the first opportunity'; that was the next day as the conditions would be suitable. The battle that was to begin on 22 April had its origin in a strong desire to make a thorough trial of gas as a weapon at the front after successful trials in the homeland. There was no follow-up planned; if the gas was a success, then ammunition could be allocated from time to time as the need arose. It was eventually decided that *XXVII. Reserve Corps* could use the gas to improve its positions by a thrust towards the line Zonnebeke-Gravenstafel but, as the conditions were never correct, the attack was moved to the front held by *46 Reserve Division* and *XXVI. Reserve Corps*.

As final preparations were being made to disperse the gas over two mediocre French divisions, a prisoner from *234 Regiment* of *XXVI. Corps*, taken at Langemarck on the night of 14 April, told his interrogators that an attack in the salient had been scheduled for the night of 15/16 April and that the attack would use an asphyxiating gas released from tubes in the ground. In his possession was cotton waste in a gauze bag which could be dipped in a solution to counteract the effects of the gas. The prisoner also told his French captors that morale was good and that they expected little opposition, but that the attack would be postponed if the wind was not in the right direction. Fortunately the French did not believe him, thinking he was a plant to take their attention off other sectors.

The construction of billets required large amounts of timber so saw mills were taken over to produce planks. The picture shows a newly-felled tree trunk being moved ready for sawing into planks.

Passchendaele church in 1915, showing the damage caused by Allied shelling.

The next day the RFC was unable to verify any aspect of the prisoner's story. Two days later an increase in rolling stock at Wervicq indicated the possible arrival of reinforcements, but there was still no proof. Belgian sources indicated the mass production of the cotton and gauze mouth protectors but, as no attack materialised, no further notice was paid to the information; the French regarded it as a ruse to stop them sending troops to the Arras front or as an attempt to inspire terror. The British moved two battalions closer to the front and kept troops relieved from duty close to the front, but this was quickly forgotten at the start of the fighting at Hill 60 and the bombardment of Ypres by a seventeen inch howitzer. The huge shells 'travelled through the air with a noise like a runaway tramcar on badly laid rails. Having delay-action fuzes, they formed immense craters.' As a result of the bombardment, the evacuation of the town began.

The bombardment of Ypres and the threat of a gas attack were quickly forgotten by the British when Höhe 60 was attacked on 17 April. This mound, rather than a hill, was the result of a railway cutting nearby, where the Comines-Ypres railway passes through Ypres ridge; there two other ridges close by, also as a result of the railway.

Situated on the crest of the ridge, all three mounds provided all-round observation over the area, but especially towards Ypres and Zillebeke. The highest of the three, Höhe 60, had been captured from the French on 10 December 1914 by *39 Division* of *XV. Corps*. Although it provided an observational advantage, the British did not try to take the position until 17 April, when, after a very quiet and sunny day, without a shot being fired by either side, the British exploded two pairs of mines at 1905 hours and a single one at ten second intervals, followed by a bombardment of British field and heavy artillery on the area, accompanied by French and Belgian artillery shelling all the approaches to the area. Within two minutes of the explosion, British troops had taken the crater and the remains of any trenches; surprise was complete, the destruction almost total. Of the few survivors of *172 Regiment*, those that resisted were bayoneted; the remainder surrendered.

While the British consolidated, the retaliatory shelling began; erratic at first, it soon concentrated on the railway cutting south of the hill, the trenches nearby and the artillery battery positions with lachrymatory gas shells.

Der Kaiser im Gespräch mit General von Fabeck,
in der Mitte Kriegsminister von Falkenhayn

The Kaiser (left) in conversation with General von Fabeck Commander of *Fourth Army*. In the centre is von Falkenhayn, Commander in Chief of the Army.

As the British were relieving their troops during the night, three counter-attacks were launched around midnight with a further one just before dawn. By 0830hours, some of the defenders had been so overwhelmed by high explosive and gas, probably due to shells exploding on the gas cylinders dug into the hill ready for the attack, and machine-gun fire in enfilade, that they had been forced back from parts of the crest. There ensued a heavy day of fighting and shelling that petered out during the night. The next day the British positions were shelled but not attacked.

Furious fighting recommenced on 20 April, mainly by bombing (grenade throwing), followed by full infantry attacks at 1830 hours and 2000 hours. These were not successful, and further attacks were carried out the next day. By this time the trenches no longer existed. Höhe 60 'was a medley of confluent mine and shell craters, strewn with broken timber and wire: and in this rubbish heap it was impossible to dig without disturbing the body of some British or German soldier.' Fierce close combat continued on Höhe 60

There was considerable air activity on the Flanders front with the majority of crashes being recorded as a record of success for the air force. This photo shows the remains of a French plane near Ypres.

A private photo showing some of the damage to the Cloth Hall.

and, by 5 May, it was again entirely in German hands. Fortunately no gas cylinders were discovered by the British, so the weapon was still a secret.

The objective, issued by *Fourth Army* on 8 April, was the capture of Pilckem Ridge and the ground adjoining it on the east. On 14 April it was extended to securing the line of the Yser Canal as far as Ypres, but there was still no allotment of reserves to *Fourth Army* by the Supreme Command before the attack; none would be made at any point during the battle which was to last into May.

As 22 April was a glorious spring day, aerial reconnaissance by the British showed considerable movement behind the lines, including a column on the march through Houthulst Forest, but nothing out of the usual. Heavy shelling of Ypres by eight and seventeen inch howitzers plus field pieces, and the mid-day shelling of the approach roads into the town, gradually died down, raising no concerns among the British staff.

'Several senior army commanders did not share Falkenhayn's faith in gas warfare. Crown Prince Rupprecht...informed Falkenhayn and Haber that he considered the plan both morally and militarily questionable. If the operation proved successful, the Allies, with their superior industrial plant, would quickly copy it.' As the prevailing winds came off the sea, the British would be able to use gas ten times more often than the German Army could.

215 Reserve Infantry Regiment received its orders at midnight on 21/22 April; 'respirators were then examined to see if they were damp, sandbags removed from the gas cylinders, and the tubes laid over the parapet; sortie steps were made, the ladders available divided, and passages cut in the wire by the engineers. At 5.20 a.m. orders were received that the attack would begin at 5.45 a.m. At 5.30 a.m., however, there being no wind the attack was postponed.' Already packed in their trenches waiting to attack, the troops could do nothing but wait; fortunately there was no artillery fire. Then 'as the sun began to set a wind got up, and at 4.40 p.m. definite orders were issued for the opening of the cylinders at 5 p.m.' The die was cast.

Then, at 1700 hours, the peace was broken by a new and furious bombardment of Ypres by heavy howitzers, followed by the heavy shelling of the relatively untouched villages in front of Ypres. Although the French field artillery retaliated, they received no counter-battery fire. Leaving the gas cloud to spread, it would be ten minutes before shrapnel fire would be initiated and twenty minutes before the troops would advance on the French positions.

Two greenish-yellow clouds spread across the ground on either side of Langemarck towards the French positions. Moving in the light wind, the clouds joined up to become a blueish-white mist; following behind were the attacking troops. Almost immediately the French soldiers were pulling back, to be followed by some of the French artillery and, although some remained in position and continued to shell the attacking force, they had all fallen silent by 1900 hours.

Almost all the Algerian troops and Territorials were in flight but the Tirailleurs on the right of the attack, the Canadians next to them and the Zouaves in reserve held their positions. The attacking troops pressed on fast through the gap created by the French withdrawal and were soon within 300 or 400 yards of the Poelcapelle to St. Julien road. There they were held up by two platoons of the 13th Canadians, who fought until their last man fell, and a company of 14th Canadians. The firing of the guns of two Canadian batteries north of St. Julien halted the advance by 1830 hours.

While the Canadians were taking stock and moving troops to fill the gap in the line, a further successful attack at 2100 hours was launched on the Tirailleurs, who gave way, although some managed to join up with the Canadians. By the end of the attacks, there were no formed bodies of French troops east of the canal except at Steenstraat, the French had no flank at Pilckem and, along with their field guns, had abandoned their first and second line; British field pieces in Kitchener's wood, in the French area, had to be abandoned but were captured without their breechblocks and strikers. The gap created was 8,000 yards wide, leaving the way to Ypres open, but the attacking force received orders to halt and dig in; by 2030 hours the front was quiet.

The Belgian positions had not been attacked during the day but the troops had seen the gas cloud and made preparations in case the assault changed direction, which it did at around 1930 hours. *46 Reserve Division* attacked across the canal but were repulsed, as was the follow-up attack after a gas bombardment. The attack focus then changed to two British divisions that were assaulted just after midnight, again with no success.

Brave troops inspect a large unexploded aircraft bomb dropped on a rear area camp by British planes.

A wooden bridge constructed over the Yser Canal by pioneers to replace the stone bridge destroyed by Belgian troops in their retreat. The card was sent by Landsturmmann Eppenberger in *Landsturm Infantry Battalion Heilbronn* to his wife and children in Böckingen near Heilbronn.

Throughout the night the bombardment of Ypres continued, as did the shelling of the approach roads and small villages. Shell-fire on the Ypres to Boesinghe road was so intense as to make it practically impassable.

Further east, the Canadians were counter-attacking towards Granat Waldchen with complete success, but the French troops achieved nothing. So although the wood had been passed through and prisoners from *234 Reserve Infantry Regiment* had been taken, the position was untenable and, when a supporting company was exterminated the next day, the position was evacuated. However, for all the success of the attacks, inertia allowed the Allies to find enough troops to plug the gap.

At the end of the day *45 Reserve Division* had fought hard for possession of Steenstraat, and the village was taken only late in the evening and the attacking troops failed to get beyond the western exit of the village. 'The advance of the *6th Reserve Division* against the Ypres canal was likewise difficult; but late in the evening it reached the canal everywhere, and at Het Sas, passed through it. The left flank got only as far as the steam mill east of Boesinghe. The advance of the *XXVI. Corps* succeeded best. In particular, the *52nd Reserve Division*, as early as 5.30 p.m. reached Pilckem and the Haanebeek' (Steenbeek); but was ordered thirty minutes later not to go beyond the southern slope.

In some areas the gas was more effective than others. It was more suited to open spaces, so it did not have the same effect on the defenders of the Langemarck ruins, nor on the sides of the road from Poelcapelle to Keerselare, thus making progress for *51 Reserve Division* more difficult than for its close neighbours. However, by 1800 hours, the division had passed through the village and moved on towards the Haanebeek, with orders to capture the bridgehead prior to attacking St. Julien.

At the end of 22 April, progress had been made, but not in a major way. The official government communiqué issued the next day did not mention the gas: 'Yesterday we broke out of our front Steenstraat-Langemarck against the enemy position north and north-east of Ypres. In one rush our troops pressed forward on a nine-kilometre frontage to the heights south of Pilckem, and eastwards of them. At the same time, after a stubborn fight, they forced the passage of the Ypres canal at Steenstraat and Het Sas, where they established themselves on the western bank'.

General von Einem, commander of *Third Army* in Champagne, had, before the attack,

Older soldiers were often used as garrison or service troops. Here a group of Landsturm soldiers pose in and in front of their lorry, inscribed 'in remembrance of the campaign in Belgium 1915.' The Landsturmmann's most distinguishing feature was his oilcloth cap (Wachstuchmütze) with its metal Landwehr Cross. Although they served a vital military purpose in the army, they were frequently issued old and out-dated uniforms, equipment, and weapons.

given his verdict on its use: it would cause a 'tremendous scandal in the world'. The day after the release of chlorine at Ypres, he wrote to his wife: 'The higher civilization rises, the more vile man becomes.' The two men who were mostly deeply involved with the project, Haber and Tappen, both chemists, were rewarded by a grateful Kaiser. The former received the Iron Cross first class and the latter was promoted to major-general.

'Though a local success, gas rapidly became a propaganda gift to the enemy.' However, it would not be long before this was forgotten and the same gas would be used by the Allies, as Rudolph Binding observed after surveying a battlefield where it had been used: 'The effects of the successful gas attack were horrible. I am not pleased with the idea of poisoning men. Of course the entire world will rage about it at first and then imitate us. All the dead lie on their backs with clenched fists; the whole field is yellow.'

The battle would continue through April and into May but no extra troops would be supplied by Supreme Command at any time. *Fourth Army* had limited reserve troops so, throughout the fighting, it was continually forced to move troops around its sector, thus providing fresh troops while maintaining its own sector.

The previous day's attacks had left the French in poor state; they had lost most of their artillery, and had received very few reinforcements; they were therefore unable to attempt to regain lost territory. Fortunately for them, the front was initially quiet, giving the British time to improve their positions and, in the early morning, the British and Canadian troops launched an attack against the deepest penetration from 22 April in order to solidify their line. Resistance was tough and British casualties were high. There was some success in joining up the positions but a gap still existed between the British and the French. It was then the British realised that their seventeen and a half battalions were being opposed by forty two German ones.

Although the British attacks were resisted strongly, no counter-attacks were under-taken, although ordered, except on the French front where position improvements were

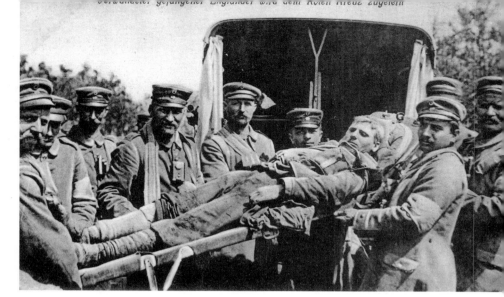

A wounded British soldier is taken away by trained medical personnel who pose happily for the camera.

made on the west bank of the canal, and on the Belgian sector where an attempt to cross the canal by boat and raft failed. The shelling of Ypres continued, often with gas, throughout the day.

In the afternoon the French launched a counter-attack, as did the British, but little progress was made against the strong defence. Similarly attacks on the French made no progress but the bridgeheads at Het Sas and Steenstraat and the ground between them were held.

After the war a writer for the Reichsarchiv summed up the situation, explaining why there had been so little activity: 'However desirable it was to exploit the success [of the 22nd], reserves to do so were lacking; any further advance would have involved the troops in close fighting in the dark and on unknown ground. It would have been better on the 23rd to have pursued only one objective and thrown the enemy over the Yser. The attack would have been very different if the attack [on the 22nd] had been made in

English corpses in a newly captured trench in Flanders in the early autumn of 1915. A German soldier is investigating the trench in the background. A card sent by Hugo to Klara in Zwickau.

the early morning.' Having two divergent objectives and allowing the enemy to dig in 500 yards from the front of *XXVI. Reserve Corps* and not attacking them were other reasons for the lack of success. The day was succinctly summed up by the writer: 'No further progress was made.'

The war diary of *XXIII. Reserve Corps* laid the blame on the shoulders of the soldiers involved: 'Unfortunately the infantry had become enfeebled by trench warfare and had lost its daring and indifference to heavy losses and the disintegrating influence of increased enemy fire effect. The leaders and the brave-hearted fell, and the bulk of the men, mostly inexperienced reinforcements, became helpless and only too inclined to leave the work to the artillery and trench mortars.'

Early morning RFC reconnaissance discovered little to indicate anything out of the ordinary, except an increase of trains at two railheads which could have brought reinforcements but could just as easily have been for evacuating the wounded. However, the British in the sector closest to the two railheads were put on attack footing to counter any planned German attack. Before they were ready, *XXIII. Reserve Corps*, having captured Lizerne from the French during the night, attacked the defensive flank of the Belgians at 0300 hours 'backed up by a large quantity of gas shell'. Not only did the Belgian troops hold the attack but pushed the attackers back.

Subsequently, after an hour's heavy bombardment with guns and trench mortars, cloud gas was released against Canadian troops on an approximately thousand yard front. 'Behind the gas followed the attacking waves of the *4th Reserve Ersatz Infantry Regiment,* which was supported by the rest of its brigade and a composite brigade of the *53rd Reserve Division…*A brigade of the *51st Reserve Division* and the *4th Marine Brigade* menaced the north-western face of the apex, the right of the attack extending across the Steenbeck'. The fighting was hard and little real progress was made.

Although the fighting was very fierce, there was still time for compassion on the part of the attackers. A British-born Canadian was in the trenches when the gas arrived. He survived thanks to the kindness shown by a German infantryman. Lance Corporal Finnimore later recounted the incident: 'That day, 24 April, was the worst day of my life.

A soldiers' bar and shop. The range of goods available is very limited but does include sausage.

A postcard showing a church parade and service in Moorslede. The card was sent from a soldier in *Field Hospital 11*, a medical unit in *XXVII Reserve Corps*.

It started with a really violent bombardment and then – you could only call it a cloud of death when the gas came over, and this time it was directed straight at us. People were suffocating, but some were worse affected than others and the word was passed down that we were to hold on at all costs.' Holding on as ordered he was hit in the leg and was unable to move when ordered to retire. When he regained consciousness a German soldier was standing over him with a bayonet at his chest. His already grievous situation had worsened: he found he couldn't get up, walk or defend himself. He looked up at his opponent, expecting to be bayoneted any minute. Instead he saw the German soldier hand his gun to a comrade, disappear in the direction of the nearby deserted farmyard, and return a few minutes later with a wheelbarrow. Finnimore was placed in it and pushed a mile or so to a dressing station where he was handed over to the medical staff.

The Reichsarchiv stated that: 'the attack encountered strong opposition and progressed but slowly. Keerselare, from which enemy machine guns were fired, held out particularly long. In the farms and hedges round St. Julien, too, the enemy resisted stoutly in spite of heavy artillery bombardment'. Some troops did eventually enter St. Julien but a strong counter-attack compelled *51 Reserve Division* to retire. The official bulletin for 24 April again did not mention gas; 'The ground gained north of Ypres on the 23rd [*sic*] was held yesterday [24th] against enemy attacks. Further to the west we continued our attacks, stormed Solaert Farm [Oblong Farm], as well as St. Julien and Keerselare and pressed forward victoriously against Gravenstafel'.

'It had been a day of close shaves.' The German Army was on the move and St. Julien had been captured. On the British side, the guns were retreating and every man was in the line. 'At nightfall the Canadians were ordered to retire from their hard-pressed front to a position further back'. As they left, their opponents immediately took their place. It was not over yet; the battle would start again the next day.

The next day, Sunday 25 April, in a mist, the British attacked in the Wieltje and St. Julien area. They immediately came under rifle and machine-gun and sniper fire from the rye grass and other crops. As they advanced, the British troops were machine-gunned from houses in St. Julien, the upper floors of farm buildings, and from the nearby woods.

A card showing marine infantry in Flanders. It was sold to raise funds for war-invalided sailors and marines. Sold for ten Pfennig, three of which went to the charity.

In St. Julien, *51 Reserve Division*, finding the village unoccupied, was making preparations for a further advance but had to quickly adjust to a defensive role, deluging the attackers with such heavy machine gun fire that they withdrew behind any cover they could find. The British were pinned down but no attempt to exploit this success, except for a weak company attack, was made.

The British 28 Division, occupying positions on a spur between the main Ypres Ridges and the Stroombek, were next to be attacked. As the British 10 Brigade was beginning its assault at 0500 hours, the British 85 Brigade found itself under organised fire, sweeping and searching the slopes of the spur with shrapnel for four hours. This changed to a heavy bombardment with gas shell and high explosive, the former having a considerable effect on the British troops. At 1300 hours the attackers left their positions and broke through British positions between the top of the ridge and the railway cutting. The hand-to-hand fighting made artillery support by either side impossible. While the attack on the right and centre faltered, on the left flank sixty yards of breastwork were occupied and successfully held against counter-attacks during the night. To prevent any further progress, the British dug a trench round three sides of their lost trench.

During the day, men of the *Marine Corps*, clad in blue, were involved in the fighting as part of the late afternoon attack to take Boetleer's Farm. This attack failed, but the British and Canadian troops were forced to pull back, while troops attempting to reinforce the position were caught in accurate artillery fire and could not get through.

In other sectors, where the distance between the lines was too great, the attacking force could not close upon the British and no progress was made. However, the attacks necessitated a reorganisation of the British lines and, while troops were attempting to rejoin their units, they were attacked. One unit falling back to the Haanebeek recorded that some of the attackers were wearing khaki though the British Official History notes that this was unlikely. The British Official History acknowledges that mistakes were made about the use of each other's uniforms; it quotes one occasion when it was claimed that Highland kilts were worn; these turned out to be the attackers' own greatcoats.

The weather had been persistently unfavourable for aerial reconnaissance, but a few

Two ageing members of the Flanders marine artillery.

flights were made by British planes. Nothing unusual was located in the immediate vicinity. On the other hand twice the number of trains had passed through Tourcoing, and news from Holland indicated that 125 train loads of troops had passed through Liège on the previous two days, more than had passed through in a similar period in 1914. The increased train movements suggested to the British that a large-scale action was in preparation, but prisoners indicated that only two Landwehr regiments had been brought up as reinforcements, and that these were there to dig trenches, while *44 Reserve Division,* which had been relieved by the *Marine Corps,* was to do the same.

While some small progress had been made against the British, none had been made against the French, where the attacks were stopped under the orders of *Fourth Army.* Unless the French regained what they had lost, Allied HQ believed that the Ypres salient might no longer be defensible. They also believed that further attacks, with the specific aim of making an Allied offensive impossible, would occur.

Throughout the day, shells landed on Ypres, destroying buildings and their contents. A Belgian priest, Father Delaere, recounted what the town looked like that day: 'The Grand Place, the Leete, the surroundings of the Cloth Hall and the Rue de Dixmude were like an abandoned battlefield. Five horses, an overturned ammunition wagon, a shattered motor ambulance, clothes scattered around, a big bundle of blankets, three bodies – a soldier and two women lying, spread out miserably, on the stones covered with dirt beside the pavements shattered and shell-holed.' 'Ypres crumbled and blazed, but for every shell that fell on the town a score were falling in the salient.'

The next day, 26 April, the artillery of the Lahore Division took up position to support a British attack, at 1405 hours, in the general direction of Langemarck. Attacking over the scene of fighting three days earlier, the troops ascended a gentle rise to Hill Top Ridge, then crossed a shallow valley before attacking the gentle slopes of Mauser Ridge held by German infantry. However, directly the attacking force crossed Hill Top Ridge, they came under heavy artillery fire, losing whole platoons at a time. Two British battalions in the Indian division made it to within about 100 yards of the German lines before they came to a standstill.

Five minutes before the start of the British attack, the French had left their support

Im Schützengraben

Captioned 'In the trenches' the card shows well-constructed living quarters in a rear area. Although winter is depicted in the photo the card was sent in July by member of 3 *Kompanie Landsturm Infanterie Bataillon I Altona* to a friend in Altona.

trenches, with two divisions following an hour later because of difficulties with artillery registration. A release of gas twenty minutes after the start held all the attackers back until it blew away. Although the attack was renewed, the defenders eventually forced the French to retire to their support line. However, the German infantry did not take advantage of this success and were attacked again at 1900 hours by black French troops who made such a noise that they drew heavy fire and made no real progress.

A further British attack fared even worse than that of the Lahore Division; its advance was over unknown ground, with insufficient ammunition, through gaps in the main defensive wire belts and under heavy artillery fire. Two lines of soldiers in artillery formation marched across the flat terrain into artillery fire and heavy machine gun fire from a wood that was not under attack. The attackers lost, in total, over two-thirds of their strength.

On Gravenstafel ridge, sometime between 0100 and 0200 hours, before the British had launched their attacks, the defending British troops were surprised to see, in the

French and Belgian enlisted men under guard while waiting for transport to take them to Germany.

A Field Postcard showing troops practising the charge in mass formation. As the soldiers were so close together, enemy machine gun fire resulted in many casualties during such an attack.

misty moonlight, a large body of men advancing towards them, calling out that they were Royal Fusiliers. Surprise was lost when an officer detected a foreign accent and opened fire. The attackers withdrew but, when the mist cleared, the area was overwhelmed with fire for the remainder of that day and for the next consecutive eight.

By the end of the day neither British nor Germans had bettered their position. There was little activity during the night; for the second night running, British troops were able to walk about in front of their lines. Facing them were troops busy digging and strengthening their trenches. Unknown to the British, the sound of digging was the installation of gas cylinders. This installation had actually started on 24 April and took several days to complete. It had been intended for use in an attack shortly after completion, but unfavourable weather conditions postponed the attack until 2 May. In the interval there was no cessation of activity on the front. Attacks and enemy counter-attacks alternated with German local offensives. In particular, there was little rest on the right flank of the *XXVII. Reserve Corps.*

Troop quality was once again mentioned in corps' documents. When the French had taken Lizerne a break-through was feared and a counter-attack was ordered; the regiment detailed for it, *204 Reserve Infantry,* would not attempt it. *XXIII. Reserve Corps* noted in its diary that 'The infantry again evidently lacks the right offensive spirit'. As the enemy seemed superior in numbers, the corps commander decided to retire the front line.

The Allied troops in the reduced salient were now covered by guns that were capable of making their position extremely uncomfortable at the least. It was difficult, acknowledged the British Official History, for the enemy 'to avoid hitting something or somebody with every shell.'

Further Allied attacks followed the next day with no success, leaving them in the same position as they had been in the morning. Casualties for the day had been very heavy.

Shelling of all parts of the salient continued throughout the night. Only one small attack was made by the British in an attempt to recover a lost trench. This was repulsed with heavy losses during the early hours of 28 April. Although the shelling continued, there followed a few days' lull in the fighting.

The gun crew of a field artillery piece pose proudly with their gun somewhere on the Flanders front. On the right is a dugout with a gas curtain hanging at the side of the entrance.

Concerted pressure on the salient had led to thoughts of retirement to a more defensible line. The planned withdrawal would abandon an area about five miles across at the base, a mile deep near Hooge and two and a half miles deep near Frezenberg. The decision was postponed, awaiting the results of the French attacks. Leaving their trenches at 1530 hours, they found the defenders prepared, and, in spite of heavy losses, they did not get within 500 yards of them. That night both sides worked on their defences. It was a clear moonlit night and the British could see their enemy busily engaged in wiring on the skyline, yet neither side disturbed the other.

French attacks the next day, 29 April, were postponed until at 1800 hours an attack on Steenstraat gained possession of the village but did not push the defenders over the canal. Even though there had been some limited success, preparations went ahead for the withdrawal.

The bombardment of the salient was almost continuous but there were no attacks on Allied positions. However, the French continued to attack but made little or no progress. Even so, the retirement was again postponed, this time at the request of General Foch.

Although the bombardment of the salient went on through the last days of April, Ypres was more fortunate. Quiet days were followed by quiet nights; so quiet had it become that people emerged from their cellars to try and resume as normal a life as possible. A few shops opened up and a baker managed to produce some bread.

The failure of the French to attack at 1510 hours on 1 May resulted in the issue of the retirement order. It was to start that night on the east of the salient. While the British were putting their plans into action, a severe bombardment was put down on Hill 60. This was followed, at 1900 hours, by a release of gas on a quarter mile front from less than 100 yards away. 'It shot over in thick volumes so quickly that very few of the men had time to adjust their extemporised respirators'. As the cloud reached the British trenches the German attackers opened rifle fire and attacked both flanks with bombing parties while the artillery concentrated on the approaches to the hill. Although suffering from the gas, a few of the defenders managed to get on the fire step and open rapid fire. This gave time for some reinforcements to arrive, thereby stopping the attackers from gaining a foothold in the trench; the defenders then withdrew.

A French postcard showing a camouflaged German heavy artillery piece.

On the Eastern Front, 2 May was the first day of a new Austro-German offensive. The Ypres front was quiet and the Allies issued orders for stage two of the retirement. However, at 1200 hours, a heavy artillery barrage was put down on the British troops holding the left wing of the salient where they linked with the French right wing. At 1600 hours this changed to gas shelling, and thirty minutes later a gas cloud was released on a three-mile front across a no man's land of, at maximum, 150 yards. Following this were troops of *XXVI. Reserve Corps*.

The gas took three minutes to reach the British positions and fifteen minutes to pass, giving the reserves time to reinforce the front line and for the French and British artillery time to lay down accurate fire on the troops following the cloud. The surprise attack had failed with heavy losses. By 2000 hours the front was quiet.

Aided by the moon and the fires burning in Ypres that illuminated the whole country-side, the troops continued their retirement.

The spasmodic shelling of the salient during the night of May 2/3 became more methodical during the day when it was joined by trench mortars. Any retaliation by British guns was quickly extinguished. Soldiers marching from Moorslede to Passchendaele were spotted, and troops cutting their wire and lying out in no man's land ready to attack were clearly observed. As they rose to advance, they were shot down by rapid accurate small arms fire from the British trenches. The attempt dwindled away. Fighting continued throughout the day as the British continued their phased retirement. The official communiqué was simple: 'Heavy British losses near Ypres.' General Balck blamed the failure of the day on his superiors for not sending reinforcements, and for the lack of fighting spirit in the men: 'Again the attack had come to a standstill, the troops' strength had not been kept up, and they were at the end of their powers'. The numbers in his *51 Reserve Division* were inadequate: his average company strength was down to 90 men; before the battle it had been somewhere between 180 to 250.

The withdrawal during the night of 3/4 May went unnoticed and without resistance. As usual the next morning the forward British trenches were shelled. In order to assist the

Hugo, a private in *107 Infantry Regiment*, poses with his fiancée Klara at home in Zwickau. His unit was part of *24 Infantry Division* that fought in Belgium in 1914 and 1915.

retirement, the French attacked in two areas at the north of the salient; the third attack made no headway because of the strength of the wire facing it.

During the morning it became obvious that the British had left their positions and troops began a cautious advance into the abandoned territory. A cavalry officer described what he saw when he went forward: 'The whole countryside is yellow…the battlefield is fearful. A curious sour, heavy penetrating smell of dead bodies strikes one…Bodies of cows and pigs lie, half decayed; splintered trees, the stumps of avenues; shell crater after shell crater on the roads and in the fields.'

Herbert Weisser, who was killed at Ypres on 25.5.15, wrote about his experiences during the advance: 'You have of course read in all the newspapers about our advance here. We are just in the most frantic corner and are the first who have broken through, away from that tedious sticking in one position. But then one sees the long, long processions of wounded; the dead bodies on the battlefields; one sees the spiritual and moral effects of war; the burning of villages and everything'.

A British trench near Ypres sometime during 1915. In the trench wall, made of sandbags, is a sniper/observation plate to allow observation of the enemy lines.

The new British positions were easily found by the air force as Private Vaughan of the Canadian Army saw: 'Next morning there wasn't a cloud in the sky and pretty soon after it got light some German planes came over looking for us, and of course they'd found we'd gone by then but they had no idea before the morning, because all night and when we were going back, we'd hear them bombarding, wasting their shells on empty trenches...When these planes came over us and spotted us they dropped smoke bars over the side of the plane, and the German artillery officers would naturally have their glasses trained on the plane...and these smoke bars came down in streaks and they just hung there above our position. No clouds, no wind to blow them away, they just hung there plumb above us – and then it started!'

Following behind the infantry and their mounted officers came the guns, which quickly opened up on the exposed British troops on Frezenberg ridge. So much damage was done to the new positions and each position was so accurately registered by the guns that the British spent the night digging new trenches behind the original one. With the fall of darkness, the British became aware of new positions being constructed opposite them across no man's land 200 to 600 yards away.

OHL reported that: 'There was again a scene of mobile warfare, which had not been witnessed for so long, as our leading lines in open order, followed by closed supports, broke in on the Flemish landscape; long trains of artillery and ammunition columns were brought up at a trot and reserves lay in the green meadows and abandoned British position. Everywhere in the devastated sector were the mighty results of our weapons to be seen.'

With no immediate opposition a rapid advance would have been expected but General Balck's units made slow progress, finding more difficulties than expected. 'Polygon Wood was traversed, Zonnebeke taken, then Nonne Bosschen; it became more and more evident that it was not a matter of rear guards at Frezenberg and Westhoek, but a forward position of the enemy, behind which stood his main forces. The German attack came to a standstill...As the day came to an end it was recognized that the new position could not be taken without a thorough artillery preparation.'

As the front line was now much closer to Ypres, the decision to evacuate the town was taken. The town was in the throes of a typhus epidemic and order was increasingly difficult to maintain. All civilians were to leave, the able-bodied by foot, the old and sick by ambulance.

Landsturman Kramer of *Landsturm Regiment 15* poses proudly with his Gewehr 88 rifle. Note the standard oilcloth cap and M1889 ammunition pouches.

A Flanders battlefield in 1915. The shell craters are filled with water, and the trees have been blown bare by explosions. In the foreground are numerous barbed wire entanglements.

Over the next three days, while the French in the north of the salient kept up the pressure on their front in order to distract attention from the Arras offensive, the British continued to strengthen their defences under bombardment. All attempts to get through the new British positions failed, and both sides suffered heavily. Hill 60, which had not been included in the retirement area, was the exception.

Described by the official British History 'as a mere rubbish heap of shell and mine-torn earth, timber and dead bodies…The British trenches were shapeless cavities; there was no other kind of shelter.' Then, on 5 May at 0845 hours, there appeared, a hundred yards away, clouds of gas. With a favourable wind, the gas drifted slowly at and then along the trenches. Coming from the flanks it stopped the British plan, if gas was released, of moving to the sides and letting the reserves fill the centre.

Further aiding the attack, the gas hung about the trenches so thickly that, even with dampened cotton respirators, the defending troops could not remain; those that did were overcome, others fled. After fifteen minutes of gas, the attacking *30 Infantry Division* advanced and 'secured all but a small portion of the front line on the lower slopes of the hill.' As the two sides fought for the possession of one trench, a further gas cloud was launched against positions nearby. The arrival of British reinforcements allowed them to counter-attack repeatedly, forcing the attackers back, and regaining many of the trenches they had lost, but not clearing the crest of the hill. Further attacks continued into the night; the British made little progress; those troops that did reach the crest were cut down by enfilade fire from the Caterpillar and Zwarteleen positions.

The next day, a weak British attack was beaten off and all the attackers killed or taken prisoner. Worn out, exhausted, both sides spent the next two days consolidating their new positions. Hill 60 would now remain relatively quiet until the fighting of June 1917.

However, the battle was not yet over. While both sides were consolidating, Duke Albrecht von Württemberg succeeded in moving his heavy artillery forwards and amassing the greater part of *Fourth Army* opposite two British divisions astride the Menin and Frezenberg roads. The British trenches were narrow and only three feet deep, due to the high water table, and fell in even without bombardment; they were difficult to defend.

England was hated by many in the German armed forces as being responsible for the war and attempting to keep Germany down as a nation. Even simple field postcards that conveyed brief messages to loved ones at home were stamped with anti-English sentiment.

During the night of 7/8 May, British troops became aware of patrols in no man's land. In the dark, the *Marine Division* assaulted positions near Mouse Trap Farm but were beaten off. At 0530 hours a very heavy localised bombardment of British positions commenced

A machine gun unit pose with their weapon – captured French light machine gun. Captured equipment was often used to make up for shortfalls in the arrival of standard equipment. 'The 8mm Hotchkiss Mle 1914 was the basic French heavy machine gun during the Great War. It functioned only on automatic, was gas operated and air-cooled. The construction was sturdy and simple. Albeit a bit cumbersome, it was a very reliable weapon, with the only drawback being the feed method: the metallic feed trays reduced the practical rate of fire'.

and became a general bombardment by 0700 hours. By 0910 hours the greater part of the British trench parapets were flattened out and the trenches destroyed.

Little opposition could be expected. In its history, written after the war, *242 Reserve Infantry Regiment* noted that 'the effect of the heavy artillery was devastating, one shell crater ran into another…only a few desperate survivors defended themselves obstinately.' However few in number, the defenders did not retire when the attacking infantry rose from the trenches opposite to begin their assault. The first attack was driven off as was the second after a further thirty minute bombardment. By this time practically all of the defending troops in the front line had been killed, wounded or buried and there was no hope of their reinforcement. A third assault was more successful, coming as the British received orders to retire to their support lines; any further advance was halted by determined British resistance. Across the whole of the new front the fighting was heavy and losses were high on both sides.

Pushing up reserves from the canal area, the British launched an evening attack which successfully dislodged the new occupants of Hill 33, pushing them back towards Frezenberg. This unexpected assault had the effect of putting *Fourth Army* on a defensive footing and forcing two of the three corps who had sustained the attack to abandon their newly captured positions. No further attempts to break the British positions were made for five days, though British positions were constantly attacked on a local level whenever an area had been swept clear of defenders by the artillery. Throughout the night, stragglers made their way back to the British lines.

Further south in French Flanders and in Artois, the British and French launched their own offensives, while staying on the defensive at Ypres. Over the period from 9 to 11 May, further attacks were launched on the Menin Road area held by the British 27 Division; British 4 Division positions were assaulted and the whole of the salient was bombarded at certain hours. Although gas was used, the defenders' respirators proved sufficient to allow them to remain in position. In some positions, the state of the ground and artillery-felled trees hampered movement on both sides.

On 11 May, after a 3½ hour bombardment, massed infantry again attacked British

Zonnebeke in late 1915. Virtually every house has sustained a greater or lesser degree of damage.

positions along the Menin Road. In this assault the gas blew back into the advancing attackers, exposing them to heavy machine gun fire, causing severe casualties. However, another bombardment completely destroyed the British trenches, forcing them to withdraw to their support line. This allowed the attacking troops to seize the highest point, 55 metres high, at the bend of the Menin Road and Sanctuary Wood. 'A fight with alternate attack and counter-attack went on well into the night for the possession of this locality', but the British could not take it back.

The following day, apart from the normal heavy bombardment, was uneventful on both sides. From 0330 to 1300 hours, the trenches and back areas were bombarded incessantly, and after that intermittently until nightfall. The front between Hooge and the Ypres-St. Julien road received the heaviest bombardment. Shrapnel and high-explosive coupled with incessant rain turned the British trenches into a quagmire, allowing troops to break into positions held by dismounted cavalry and bomb them out. Dismounted cavalry in the support line, firing into the newly vacated line, stopped the attacking troops from following on. As no further advance was possible, the assault force started building a firing line opposite the British support troops.

A Home Front propaganda card: Kaiser Wilhelm, his son Crown Prince Wilhelm and grandson Prince Wilhelm. In May 1940, grandson Wilhelm was wounded during the fighting in Valenciennes in France and died in a field hospital in Nivelles on 26 May 1940.

Further attacks took place, none of which greatly altered the positions of either side. Attack was met with counter-attack and more artillery fire. British troops counted 100 shells a minute landing on Mouse Trap Farm, resulting in the annihilation of the two platoons holding it. The farm was then occupied by the attacking troops, only to be lost again in the evening to a counter-attack.

The ferocity of the fighting is shown by the casualty totals for such a short period. Five British divisions recorded total losses of 9365 officers and men. Over the period 20 April to 11 May, two reserve divisions saw their total strength cut from 27,230 officers and men down to 18,417. A shortage of ammunition caused by the needs of *Sixth Army*, under attack in France, and the need to rest the troops of *Fourth Army* attacking round Ypres, meant that the 1915 Battles of Ypres were soon to end with attacks by the French against the west bank of the Ypres Canal and others against the British on Bellewaarde Ridge.

Although minor attacks were made against British positions over the next few days, no progress was made. Heavy casualties were caused when British artillery shelled troops forming for the attack. These small-scale enterprises and desultory firing gave the British time to improve their defences, trenches, and rear positions, and allowed them to bring up reserves.

The next to undertake the offensive were the French. On 15 May, 153 Division assaulted and secured the houses on the eastern bank of the canal at Steenstraat and the bridge. The defending troops on the western bank were not dislodged until two further French divisions were thrown into the attack. Despite violent counter-attacks, the key defensive point, the farm in the south of the village, could not be held and the defenders withdrew, leaving their dead behind. 'The French were now in complete possession of the western bank, and the Belgians in their original position.'

After a quiet night, British troops stood to at 0215 hours, 24 May, just in case of attack. At 0245 hours they saw four red lights, then two more, followed by heavy fire from artillery, machine guns and rifles. Simultaneously a cloud of gas was released against British positions on a 4½ mile gas front: the biggest so far. The British Official History recorded that as the wind was light the gas cloud moved very slowly, 'and from the air seemed almost stationary over the trenches. They rose 40 feet high from the ground and were so dense as to blot out houses; in the course of time their effect was felt twenty miles behind the line, and, it is recorded, was still very bad on the canal bank at 6 A.M.'

Defending trenches knee-deep in mud, their sides collapsing, and under a 4½ hour bombardment, the British defenders managed to slow down or in some cases hold the assaulting troops. However, pressure on the defenders continued to mount through the day, although 'the troops were at the end of their powers'. Then at 1700 hours the British counter-attacked.

Though initially successful in taking some of their objectives, not all of the British troops could reach their start lines at the same time. The late afternoon attack became a late evening assault, which despite the bright moonlight managed to get within a few yards of their target trenches without severe losses. However, 'they were forced back by rifle and machine-gun fire at point-blank range', suffering heavy casualties.

Not everything went well for the defending troops. One small British operation met with success. Two companies sent to drive the defenders out of houses along the Menin Road succeeded in their objective, with the escaping defenders 'running back in the dark and being fired upon by their own people.'

To the north of the salient, at the junction of the French and British positions, a French attack had failed to materialise. This left a large gap for a small number of tired British troops to re-take. Much of the ground was classed as indefensible because it was water-logged, and accordingly, after removing their wounded, the British pulled back to new positions under cover of the night. That evening *Fourth Army* ordered the end of major operations.

The next day, 25 May, passed without attacks by either side and only limited shelling of British positions. Minor actions continued through the month with the British retaking Hooge village, the château stables, pushing their positions out to the north of Hooge and consolidating them. Nothing decisive had been achieved because there were no reserves to exploit any breakthrough. Both sides were tired and short of shells but 'raids and mining did not cease on either side.'

'Despite the new gas weapon, the success of the action at Ypres did not extend past the initial gains. The objective of closing the Ypres Salient was not accomplished, mainly because on 22 April the element of surprise could not be sufficiently exploited owing to the approaching darkness. By early May the enemy had retreated to prepared positions between Wieltje and Little Zillebeke; there, despite losses, it repeatedly attacked *XXVI* and *XXVII. Reserve Corps*. The initial successes north of Ypres were mostly due to the employment of gas. This demonstrated to the commanders and rank and file its use as a new weapon, despite its shortcomings.'

It is not possible to compare casualty rates directly because German casualties who stayed in their corps area were not included on casualty lists. Using official figures the comparative figures are: British – 59275 officers and men; German 34873 – all ranks.

This second Battle of Ypres had been 'another murderous campaign for even less purpose on the German side than their enemy.' These heavy losses were incurred in order to test a new weapon and fabricate a misleading deception to cover up plans for an offensive in the east; they drained an already overstretched manpower pool.

One solution to make up the deficiency was to use a cadre of twenty-five per cent seasoned troops in each division and to start reducing the number of men in each, culminating in the divisions becoming triangularised. Instead of four brigades each would have three, hence one new division could be produced from every already-existing three.

'East of Ypres the line had settled down.' The British had lost the advantage, losing the whole of Bellewarde Ridge and north of the Menin Road. 'The skeleton of Ypres was in full view and, although the battle had died down, the guns never ceased to shell it…Ypres was a dead city.'

While the focus of the fighting on the Western Front changed and no further major actions were to take place in Flanders until 1917, it was never a quiet front, although it was an area used by both sides to rest troops. During the remainder of the year, Ypres and the salient continued to be shelled; on the busiest single day, 3000 shells were fired. All operations were of a minor nature and equally initiated by both sides.

Nearly a year on, to most soldiers, the war was neither exciting nor an adventure. Many saw it as something to be endured, something to try to survive, while constantly hoping for it to end. For Kurt Rohrbach, a theology student at Stettin at the outbreak of war, it was a time of loss; loss within himself, and also the death of his father. He expressed his loss to a friend, in a letter at the end of July. 'In this war…I feel that I have lost many of the treasures amassed during a period of gradual, auspicious development, in time of peace. The knowledge which I acquired at school and at the University, the interests aroused in me by a civilian occupation, are lost to sight and memory, and only with difficulty will it be possible to regain them'.

The need to concentrate his attention and constantly exert his strength forced Private Rohrbach to take a more serious view of life. At the age of twenty-two he felt his youth had been cut short and that he could never fall in love because of his experiences. He felt that the war had made him an old man. It may have weather-proofed his body and given him muscles as hard as iron but his mind was not developing. 'Everybody who looks daily into the cold eye of death, and gazes on so many dead faces bearing the stamp of suffering and renunciation, becomes certainly callous, but also old, very old'.

However, not all soldiers had lost their patriotism, their fervour for adventure or their belief in the justice of their country's cause. Arthur Mees, a twenty-six-year-old engineer,

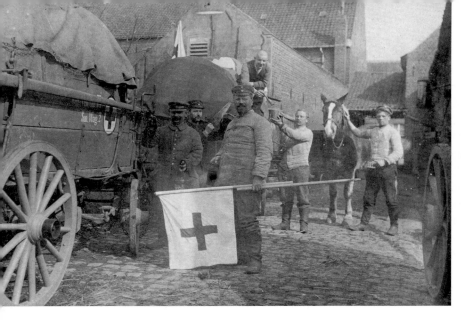

Members of *Reserve Field Hospital 78*, part of *46 Reserve Division* in *XXIII Reserve Corps*, somewhere in Belgium during April 1915. The photo was taken during a quiet period in between the fighting round Lizerne Net Sas and Steentraat, between 22 and 27 April (when the card was sent).

still believed in the hero's death. After receiving a letter from the mother of a close friend who had died he wrote: 'Oh how I wish I could press his hand once more! Those hours with him in Berlin are now doubly precious to me. But as for mourning for him – good heavens, yes, my heart aches, of course, but at this time, when our dear Fatherland is in danger greater even than that of a hundred years ago, is not every drop of blood that is shed hallowed, and has not Walter died the most splendid, the most glorious death that one can imagine? Good Lord, how I envy him, how proud I feel of him, how I long – forgive me – to shed my blood too for the dearly loved Fatherland, for Kaiser and King!' Infanterist Mees was killed near Nieuport on 24 July.

Any leave was eagerly anticipated, but home-leave was especially prized. This did not come round as often as wished; but it did not always measure up to expectation. After volunteering to retrieve a machine gun from a trench at Pilckem, Rohrbach woke up the next day to find the Sergeant-Major at his tent, telling him he had been granted eight days' home-leave. He left gladly with 'a breast full of anticipation.' In a letter he noted his joy; and the contrasts he found during his journey. Having joined a train at Houthulst, he wrote: 'the little line soon carried me away from that murderous region where the only aim of culture seems to be to devise new methods of slaughter and destruction'.

As his journey continued, the landscape was no longer barren; he saw 'fertile acres of corn, vari-coloured cattle in the meadows, and – instead of charred ruins – prosperous farm-houses, nestling among orchard-trees laden with fruit'. He noted that the people 'seemed quite unconscious of the fact that only a few miles from their homes an insane, gigantic struggle was going on'. At Courtrai, he joined the first train out, only to find it was a very slow one and would result in a fifty-one hour journey to Berlin, his home town.

Pleased to be in Germany, he drank in the sights as he crossed the country. Arriving at the suburban station near his family home, he noted that nothing appeared to have changed since his departure.

Walking briskly and full of expectation, he turned the corner of his street: 'the big front-door opened and my sister and brother came out to meet me, followed by Wölfchen, who barked loudly while they embraced me. In the doorway my dear mother put her arms round me. As soon as they released me I said, "But where's Dad?" and stepped towards the room where he had lain for months, ever since he was first taken ill. At that my mother fell into my arms: "He is dead," she said, "he died two days ago. His last words, as the doctor laid a cool hand on his burning forehead, were "There was a letter from Kurtchen (Kurt's family name) to-day" – and then he died".'

The most active months were July and September. During July, advanced Entente trenches on the Verlorenhoek road near Ypres were raided. A few days later, British troops stormed trenches between Boesinghe and Ypres. An attack on Belgian positions along the Yser Canal was repulsed and the British took the redoubt at Hooge after exploding a mine. The month ended with a successful attack, using flame throwers, by *126 Infantry Regiment* of *53 Reserve Division* on British positions on the Menin Road near Hooge, but separate British counter-attacks on 3 and 9 August resulted in their loss.

In July 'the line of brick heaps which had once been Hooge Château was in German hands, while the stables remained in the hands of the British.' Running westwards from that point, the British line crossed and re-crossed the Ypres-Menin Road through the ruins of Hooge village. 'On July 19 a mine was exploded by the British and the resulting crater which was 120 feet wide and 20 feet deep, was occupied'.

In this area, no man's land was between 70 and 150 yards wide, but at the crater it was as little as 15 yards. At one point, what had become a German communication trench led straight into the British line where it was barricaded. Using a periscope it was possible to see the sentry on duty in the opposite trench only five yards away. Attempts by the British to take the trench had been stopped with heavy fire.

On the night of 29 July, the British troops holding the Hooge Crater were relieved by comparatively inexperienced troops, new to the area, who found the crater and mining operations difficult. Using 'listening sets' gave the German soldiers full prior knowledge of the troops they were facing and their movements. The night was quiet, punctuated only by a few British bombs thrown into the German trenches; these elicited no retaliation.

Card number six in a large series designed to show those at home what the trenches in Flanders looked like. This trench section includes graves and some rather sturdy dugouts.

English Trenches near Zonnebeke captured during May 1915. A private photograph taken by one of the attackers after the battle.

The next day the British positions would be doused in liquid fire from a series of flame throwers in the trenches opposite them. This form of warfare was new in this area, but it had been tested earlier, and successfully, on 26 January against the French at Verdun. That attack was so effective that the unit was enlarged and 'soon gained battalion strength as the *Third Guards Pioneers*.'

At 0315 hours, jet upon jet of liquid fire, from the nozzles of six Flammenwerfer Apparate placed unobtrusively over the parapets, were launched over the British trench. Simultaneously a three-minute artillery bombardment landed on the same trenches. The British soldiers heard a hissing sound and then were hit by the flame and intense small arms fire. This was followed by a German attack in force. The attackers broke through the crater and then spread out left and right, bombing their way along the trenches. There were no British survivors.

14. Die Artillerie setzt über einen Fluss auf einer schnell hergerichteten Brücke.

The retreating Entente troops destroyed bridges as they withdrew. The need to bring up supply and reserves was paramount, so bridging companies quickly constructed pontoon bridges. These would be replaced when the situation stabilised and resources and time became available.

A further attempt to use the *Flammenwerfer Apparate* was not successful. No targets were sufficiently close, and the recovered British on the periphery of the attack opened fire on the crews. Although that method was not used again that day, the attack had been a success. The British now held a line along the northern edge of Zouave Wood.

The attack force 'had achieved complete surprise, and the employment of flamethrowers was not only effective within the limited area in which they were used, but also terrorised the troops in the peripheral area of the attack.' Although fire had only killed a small number of the defenders, as most had managed to duck the flame, the survivors were bayoneted by the attacking troops who followed immediately behind.

This success was part of a larger attack against the British 41 Brigade that did not achieve the same results. The positions taken on a commanding ridge left the British with no option but to counter-attack as soon as possible. That afternoon, led by survivors of the flamethrower attack, an attempt was made to retake the lost trenches. After a meagre artillery bombardment, the British troops attacked against un-located machinegun positions. 'Many were caught on the British wire, and none got more than 50 yards beyond the edge of Zouave Wood.' British casualties on 30 July were extremely heavy.

Even in the summer months the water table in many areas caused widespread problems for the occupants of trenches. After a sad home-leave, Private Rohrbach returned to Flanders where he found that his usual night-time occupation was to be 'pumping', that is pumping out the tiresome filthy water that always seemed to trickle back into the communication trench leading to the front line.

Although August was a relatively quiet month, the men still had to take care when working at night. Fortunately he was opposite French troops who were happy to have a relatively placid time. Towards midnight Rohrbach and his men were sent out with a heavy hand-pump. 'It was a lovely night. The full-moon shone in the sky and lit up the way, which on a dark night is hard to find owing to the many trenches and wire-entanglements. The Frenchies were keeping comparatively quiet, and only now and then there was the report of a rifle and a bullet whizzed by, or a missile struck a tree, ricocheted and flew on with a melancholy note. Also as it was bright moonlight very few flares went up. Far away on

To provide sufficient wood for the saw mills, special tree worker units were formed, one of which is shown here preparing a tree for transportation.

The town centre of La Bassée in late 1915.

the left, probably near Ypres, the thunder of guns growled. Otherwise all was still'. There had been little rain over the previous days and so the task was soon accomplished.

As with leave, so with food – there was never enough. Any chance to get food, even if it was dangerous, was likely to be taken – as was illustrated by the actions of Rohrbach's men after they had pumped the communication trench dry. Even with an enemy who wanted a quiet time it was dangerous to jump out of a trench. In a letter home he recalled what happened when they reached a tree full of ripe pears. 'Before I could stop them, the chaps had jumped out of the trench and begun – only 120 yards from the enemy – to pelt the tree with bits of stick and lumps of clay!' Screened only by a fine white mist, the men collected pears while the bullets whistled all about. 'In a few minutes they had got every pear off the tree, and, loaded with fruit', they started back.

Even though they had risked their lives to collect pears, they were still not expecting to find anyone else doing the same in a cornfield. However, as they crossed some open ground, they discovered some of their own men mowing in order to be able to grind some flour. Rohrbach's unit eventually moved to the Somme; there he was killed in the fighting on 6 October 1916.

During the Entente autumn offensive, 'even the German armies on the Western Front that had not been directly attacked were affected to one degree or another by other enemy actions, by increased firing activity, or by the dispatching of troops.' *Fourth Army* was no exception to this. In its sector 'the Belgians threatened the reinforced *4 Ersatz Division* with an attack on 25 September, British warships pounded Zeebrugge and the German positions near Ostend from a great range but soon retreated under the fire of the German coastal batteries, which sank one of the ships.' The British record no loss that day but the Lord Clive, a monitor, was damaged by five shells from the Tirpitz Battery on 7 September. The shelling was repeated on 19 September and along the coast on 25 to 27 and on 30 September.

'In the Ypres Salient the British launched an early-morning gas attack against the sectors of *XXVI* and *XXVII. Reserve Corps.* An infantry attack followed, but this was made only by elements of 14th (British) Division against the left flank of *54th (Württemberg) Reserve*

A card sent from Flanders by Hugo to his fiancée Klara in Zwickau. This card shows Scottish dead from an attack in the early autumn of 1915.

Division. The British succeeded in breaching the trenches located south of the Roulers-Ypres railway line – successes that were due to the effect of the heavy barrage and impressive mine explosions. By late morning, however, they had been thrown back with considerable casualties.' Several enemy attacks on *39 Infantry Division*'s front on the right flank of *XV. Corps* were repelled after close combat and heavy losses, but these were estimated at about half the number inflicted on the British.

'No other attacks followed. By late September the situation near Ypres had been settled in such a way that the *OHL* was able to relocate *53rd Reserve Division* – without *106th Reserve Infantry Brigade*, which had been assigned to *Sixth Army* – to *Army Group German Crown Prince*.'

October, partly due to poor weather conditions, was mostly taken up with artillery bombardments by both sides, but the arrival of the Canadian Corps increased trench raiding. However, in late October, *Fourth Army* proposed and *OHL* agreed to a further

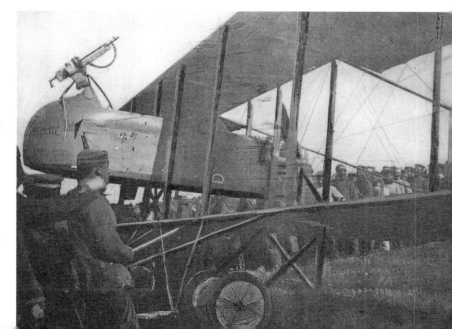

There was considerable air activity over the Flanders Front. The majority of enemy planes that crashed or landed on the German side of the wire were photographed. This is a French Maurice Farman S11 Shorthorn pusher biplane that was captured before its occupants could set fire to it.

Some distance behind the line, artillery men wait patiently for the arrival of the Goulash Cannon with their midday meal. The soldier wearing a Pickelhaube has a ball on the top rather than a point, showing him to be an gunner.

gas attack in the area east of Ypres. The commanding officer of *XXVII. Reserve Corps* pointed out that seizing 'the enemy's front line would move the troops even further into the waterlogged terrain at a most unfavourable time of year. He proposed instead an attack that would focus on the area near Wieltje with Ypres as its objective.' With insufficient resources, the attack was first postponed and then changed so that it was spread over two Corps' area.

The quietest month was November, when apart from shelling, nothing worth recording occurred. Poor weather conditions resulted in flooded trenches on the Yser front, forcing the German troops to pull back to drier ground.

December was relatively quiet. The French shelled Het Sas and the British were generally inactive. The attack postponed from October started on the morning of 19 December. Phosgene gas was released on the British north of Ypres; it caused heavy casualties but there was no panic to exploit. 'Patrols sent out from every company sector discovered that the enemy continued to occupy its trenches en masse in all places. These patrols had to withdraw in the face of the unbroken enemy position and thus sustained casualties.'

However, the year finished with a success: enemy positions near Hulluch were successfully attacked. And yet, at the conclusion of 1915, despite the cost of thousands of lives, neither side on the salient had made any major impact on the other.

Overall, at the end of the year, 'the Central Powers were unable to appear in any of the various theatres with sufficient superiority.' On the Western Front, 113 infantry divisions faced 150 of the Entente. In total, 225½ Central Powers' divisions faced 314½ enemy divisions. None of the enemies displayed any disposition toward peace and, while it had so far been possible to handle economic problems, the longer the war lasted the more threatening would the economic situation become. 'The longer the war lasted, the more the Entente would be able to bank on the fact that the Central Powers would exhaust themselves militarily and economically.'

Christmas 1915 was not a repeat of the previous year. There was still food to go round but there was no longer the feeling of goodwill to all men that had engendered the

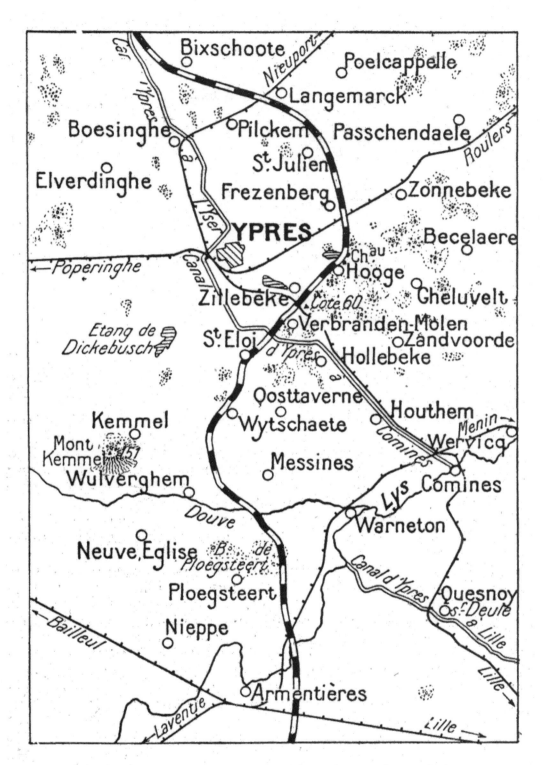

THE FRONT-LINE DURING THE WINTER CAMPAIGN OF 1914-1915.

FRÖHLICHE WEIHNACHTEN

1915-16

Die Weihnachtglocken
klingen
So feierlich und rein,
Möge ihr hehres läuten
bald Friedensläuten sein,

wünscht aus

dem Felde

Uffz. Peter

Stotzem

BELGIEN

Christmas greetings from Belgium. A card sent by an Unteroffizier in *XXVI. Reserve Infantry Corps* to a friend in Hasselsweiler, northeast of Aachen.

spontaneous truces of Christmas 1914. Although the front was generally quiet, the shelling continued. Probationer Surgeon Westman recalled one special gift that he kept for years until it broke. Every member of Crown Prince Rupprecht's Army received a large earthenware beer mug bearing a facsimile of his signature.

Stephen Westman also had another reason to remember the end of 1915. Shortly before Christmas, ambulance trains near Charleroi 'got orders to evacuate from the hospitals situated near the front line all cases of infectious or mental diseases.' They were to be taken to specially erected hutted hospitals near Cologne. After discharging its load, each train had to be disinfected. The accompanying troops were then billeted in third-rate hotels near the railway repair works to wait for their train to be ready. As the officer in charge of a hospital train, Westman had at his 'disposal whole booklets full of leave vouchers and of tickets for the railway.' He decided to make use of them and went to visit his family. Forging the signature of a non-existent colonel, he travelled twenty hours in an overcrowded train to arrive home in time for New Year's Eve.

'Despite concerns about the overall situation and the horrible sacrifices in blood that had been made to that point, the mood on the front and at home remained optimistic. Based on the clear military successes that had been achieved on the battlefield, the German people remained unshaken in their trust that the war would be brought to a positive conclusion. The initial enthusiasm for war that had been witnessed in the summer of 1914 had been replaced by tenacious determination. As 1915 made way for 1916, the will to prevail was unbroken.'

Pioneers constructing billets some distance behind the line.

The body of a Scottish Highlander in a captured British trench in Flanders. There was little censorship until much later in the war, allowing the German soldier to send home images that the British public could not see.

Although mostly shelled by artillery, Ypres was also bombed by aircraft and zeppelins.

Shell damage to a church near Ypres.

German pioneers clearing up.

The Kaiser paid many visits to the Western front. In this photograph he is accompanied by his son and two generals as they watch a divisional parade.

Courcier was Antony of Ypres' main competitor in postcard production for the area. However, Courcier covered the whole of the Western Front. This shows further damage to the town during 1915 titled: 'After the bombardment – a street in the pretty city'.

An Antony of Ypres card showing the damage the Cloth Hall sustained during the shelling of 22 November 1915. On the left is a pre-war photo for contrast.

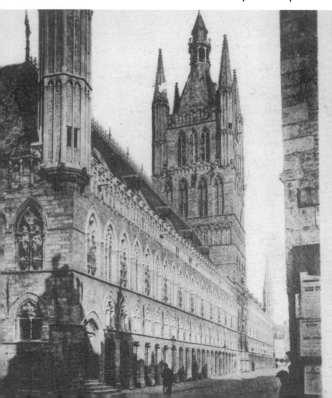

Damage caused to the church in Poelcapelle by British and French shelling.

A machine gun position in the trenches. At this angle the gun is being used for anti-aircraft defence. The card was sent to Dora by her uncle who was serving in *3 Batterie, 3 Württemberg Field Artillery Regiment 48*.

An essential job but often one given as a punishment; no one enjoys peeling potatoes in such large quantities.

A view of St. Julien to the north of Ypres showing the damage caused by British artillery. The card was sent by a soldier in *16 Reserve Division Munitions Column*, then serving in France.

An artist's version of the fighting on the Ypres Front: drums, officers on horse back and a massed charge. A card sent by a Landsturmmann in the *Heidelberg Landsturm*.

A propaganda card to show the world that the German soldier was no different to any other soldier, and certainly no barbarian.

The 'luxury' of a well-constructed Flanders trench.

A card especially produced for troops to send home. This one shows the woodland on the hills at Kemmel. Apart from a soldier in a shirt, there are no traces of the war to be seen.

„Wir Barbaren"

Ein Liebesdienst

A card sent by a soldier in *XXIII.Reserve Corps* while his unit was resting at Thourout. Again an attempt to show that the German soldier was not the barbarian the Allies suggested.

A Train Column moving to a new area. The re-location of a division required hundreds of wagons to move the equipment, causing serious congestion during the preparations for an offensive.

Behind the front – A lightly wounded officer is checked by the Watch Master while waiting to be transported to the rear.

A solidly constructed blockhouse in Polygon Wood.

Cavalry escorting newly captured British POWs to the rear, somewhere near Ypres.

A British second line trench on the Ypres front. British trenches were initially designed for temporary use so were poorly finished in comparison with German trenches.

An unusual British trench, supposedly somewhere on the Ypres Front.

A butcher's shop set up in a Brussels street.

A British plane that was shot down near Ypres. After landing safely, it became a minor tourist attraction until taken away for detailed analysis.

A German position captured during a British attack near Zonnebeke.

When men were out of the line, on rest, it was essential to check equipment before returning to the front. Here troops clean, oil and overhaul their rifles.

As the war continued, the coastal defences were increased in number: a coastal gun on the Belgian coast.

The original caption suggests that this is an armed communication trench.

In contrast to British trench construction, German troops built their dugouts to last.

A German naval aircraft taking off as an observation platform for coastal defence against British attacks.

Although bound to be unstable, with the correct engineering, dugouts could be constructed in the dunes along the Belgian coast.

Troops resting outside Ostend before moving to new positions.

Bread was an essential for all the armies on the Western Front. Here a bakery is set up in a Belgian town to provide the troops with fresh bread.

Although the life of an artilleryman seemed secure to an infantryman, it was far from safe; enemy guns targeted their opponents in counter-battery work. It was also hard work securing the gun platform, digging gun-pits, carrying ammunition and working constantly during offensives, sometimes firing so frequently that they wore their guns out.

Troops enjoying the summer weather in well-constructed reserve trenches in a wood.

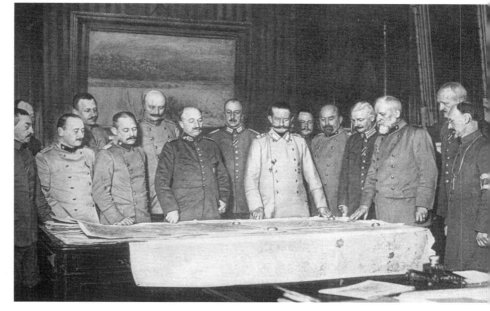

General von Bissing, Governor General of Belgium, with his staff.

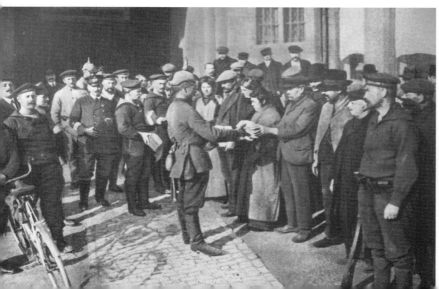

When food supplies were in short supply, the German authorities provided civilians with food from their own stocks.

As in all the combatant armies, horses were important for moving just about every item of equipment. The same railway wagon would be used to transport horses and men.

The Indian Corps had arrived in Belgium in October 1914. Unable to cope with the European weather, it was withdrawn and sent to the Middle East in December 1915. Here Indian POWs enjoy the weather before transportation to a POW camp.

Germany was an amalgam of semi-independent states, each with its own titular head. King Ludwig III of Bavaria was a frequent visitor to his troops at the front.

The remains of the church in Langemarck in 1915.

A division moving to the front prior to going into the line. The infantry are wearing shakoes instead of the more common pickelhaube.

The *Naval Corps* was tasked with defending the coast against attack from the sea in any form. Here a machine gun is sited in the dunes, prepared for an expected invasion by British troops.

Both sides laid fixed sea mines to sink ships and submarines. These often broke loose and drifted out to sea or to land. Here troops inspect some newly-arrived friendly mines.

A postcard sent home by a soldier serving outside Ypres with *39 Division*. The card shows morning toilet activities in a quiet rear position.

Mounted Algerians escort POWs to the rear.

An observation balloon unit preparing a balloon for its ascent.

Officers inspecting a trench in the dunes of the Belgian coast.

With most of Belgium occupied, the best way to keep an area secure was with cavalry.

The extent of damage to these storage tanks, destroyed during the retreat from Antwerp in 1914, is clearly shown in this 1915 picture.

As the war progressed, the defences along the coast were strengthened. Here a gun is manhandled into place to improve coastal defences.

Most movement beyond the railhead still relied on horse transport once it had left the railhead. Here provisions are being taken to a unit behind the front.

Belgium contained factories capable of producing and repairing military equipment. This is a repair depot set up by the German Army in an ordnance factory.

Roeselaere harbour before the war.

Crown Prince Rupprecht with the headquarters staff of *Sixth Army*.

Every year the Kaiser's birthday was celebrated with displays. In January 1915 it was celebrated by parades behind the front.

The Belgian ports were important to the German navy as they provided facilities for the U-boat fleet. Their closeness to Britain made them a real threat to the shipping lanes.

A 'war bridge' constructed to reduce travelling time for troops.

Troop movement was constant and railways played a large part in successfully moving troops quickly from one area to another. At each major station along the way, there was a field cooker unit to provide food.

A shortage of labour and constant use caused damage to the roads very quickly. Here a war reporter is changing the tyres on his vehicle.

Woumen near Dixmude in 1915. The damage was caused by shelling aimed to remove the observation post set up in the church tower.

The constant bombardment of Ypres made it unsafe for civilians. Those who chose to stay moved their belongings and lived their lives in the cellars during the night.

The Ypres-Comines canal was fought over on many occasions.

Chapter Two– 1916

The quietest year

'Although several powerful Entente offensives', in Italy and the Western Front, 'had dented the German lines in the west during the course of 1915, the German position remained largely the same as at the end of 1914.' Having held the Entente for over a year, the army 'looked likely to be able to hold off any similar attacks in the foreseeable future.' So 'as 1916 began, the German strategic situation was stable if not favourable.' However, Falkenhayn was no closer to achieving the goals set in November 1914.

'Through the course of 1915, the German armies had advanced deep into Russia and had seemingly crushed the Russian offensive capability. Serbia had been dealt an even heavier blow, as a combined German-Austro-Hungarian-Bulgarian force occupied the country and ejected the remnants of the Serb army from the continent. The destruction of Serbia opened rail communications with Turkey, thus helping to shore up this beleaguered ally.'

'The Italian Front had stabilised after four

Contrasting the size of a 385mm unexploded British naval shell with a rather portly Landwehr soldier.

The *53 Reserve Division's* crossroads cemetery at Broodseinde.

savage but indecisive battles along the Isonzo River. And the Allied debacle at the Dardanelles had given new life to the Ottoman Empire.'

119 divisions faced ninety-six French and forty-three British divisions and each side had built up significant reserves. In the west the German Army maintained a reserve of twenty-five divisions against a French reserve of twenty-four and three British divisions.

This balance had not been easy for the German Army to achieve and the pool of replacements was not easily filled without lowering standards. Ludendorff wrote after the war that 'the army in the field had received adequate reinforcements from returned wounded…from the yearly classes as they were called up, and from re-examinations and comb-outs', but there was still a shortfall. As a result nineteen-year-olds were called up, medical standards reduced, 'and the vast majority of the available men called up.'

To further maximise manpower, every German from 15 to 60 was obliged to serve in some way to assist the war effort. While this increased the availability of manpower, the

Men of a Landwehr regiment being decorated by Crown Prince Rupprecht in early 1916.

The British second line trenches at Ypres after an assault.

auxiliaries were paid civilian rates, a fact which caused much friction between them and the lower paid soldiers who were often doing the same job while being paid less.

Both sides had learned through bitter experience 'how difficult it was to break through a well-constructed defensive system.' The lesson was a simple one: an offensive resulted in high casualty rates, especially to the attacker, with little territorial gain. And yet, initially, there appeared to be little alternative.

The problem was further compounded. In France Falkenhayn faced two enemies, who each possessed large reserves and were dug-in behind well-constructed trenches. Both Falkenhayn and Conrad, the Austro-Hungarian General Staff Chiefs, agreed that the war needed to be ended by 1917 before both nations reached the end of their resources. Where, when and how could an attack with limited resources that would win the war be launched?

'Although Falkenhayn believed Great Britain to be Germany's main enemy, Britain was more difficult to defeat.' He believed that any major attack on the British sector would fail to force Britain out of the war and would leave Britain largely unharmed and the French Army intact. To Falkenhayn, the goal 'should be to convince Britain that it could never defeat Germany.' As a result, the decision for unrestricted submarine warfare against British shipping was made. The only way for France to be forced into peace was to destroy its army.

The achievement of this end would need an offensive that would severely weaken the French followed by a 'counteroffensive to mop up the French and British armies after they had been bled white by their own relief offensives.' Following this the Entente should fall apart, opening the way to a negotiated settlement. After the plan to attack Belfort was scrapped, another decision, to attack Verdun, was made, with the intention to bleed the French Army to death and maintain the initiative. Falkenhayn later admitted that there was never any intention of taking Verdun. As the fighting continued with no real gain, his staff began to talk about it being a second Ypres.

Strategic surprise was to be the key to success; elaborate measures were taken to ensure the secrecy of the forthcoming assault. To help cover the preparations for the

As the army in Flanders grew, so too did the need for buildings to accommodate men and store equipment. Here by the side of a railway track, men are constructing a trackside shelter.

Verdun offensive, 'Falkenhayn ordered the other armies of the *Westheer* to prepare local offensives' to deceive the Entente.

However there was to be little element of surprise. German deserters provided details of the future attack, French civilians in the occupied sector managed to get information through to Paris and the use of un-coded telephonic communication between German troop commanders provided minute detail of the forthcoming attack. Unaware of all this, the planners continued. Fortunately for them, the French intelligence service did not believe the reports and little was done to prepare the troops at Verdun.

On 6 January, the newly arrived *27 Württemberg Division* took over a two-mile section from the Ypres-Comines canal to opposite Zillebeke. At the southern end was a British held position, The Bluff. Although mining had failed previously, a larger mine was fired on 21/22 January. Again the result was the same: the British continued to overlook their positions.

Counter-battery work was undertaken by both sides on a regular basis so it was necessary both move regularly and camouflage between moves.

The view of the Ypres front from the German trenches.

There was only one option. Although an attack had been considered and rejected because of the difficulty in holding the position, the new corps commander ordered The Bluff and the trenches near it to be taken by attack. *124 Regiment* assaulted the British positions after hours of gun and trench-mortar fire and three mines between 1757 and 1759 hours on 14 February. 'In a few minutes nearly the whole enemy position was taken, and the Bluff was in the possession of the attackers.' At a few points there was desperate resistance, hard fighting and considerable losses. The Regimental History states that by 1805 hours the front line was taken and by 1832 hours the whole objective, except for one machine gun post, was in their hands.

That same day, *Fourth Army* launched an attack against the "Grosse Bastion" on the Lys Canal southeast of Ypres and *Sixth Army* renewed its assault on the Gieseler Heights, east of Souchez near Lens.

All the British counter-attacks were beaten off but with heavy losses. Between 14 and 18 February the regiment lost seventy-five killed, 229 wounded and twenty-five missing. The regiment was sent to rest, and was replaced during 20 to 22 February by *123 Grenadier Regiment*, who described the position as shot to pieces and who reported 'that the men had to cower in shell holes and bits of trench' up to their bellies in water!

In the early morning of 2 March the British attacked and regained the whole position. *124 Regiment* attributed the defeat to the defences being destroyed and the men worn out after "36 hours' continuous bombardment".' Grenadier losses are given as two officers and thirty-nine men killed, two officers and seventy men wounded and eight officers and thirteen men missing. Detachments from *124* and *127 Regiments* tried to recapture The Bluff by night attack, but abandoned the attempt. For the remainder of the war *124 Regiment* never forgave its sister regiment for losing the position it had taken.

The Verdun offensive has two links to the Ypres Front. Some of the super-heavy artillery pieces that shelled Liège, Namur, Maubege and Antwerp were also used to shell the Verdun forts and, as a result of one of the diversionary attacks, British troops were sent from Flanders to the Arras Front.

The Verdun offensive opened on 21 February accompanied by a diversionary-corps

King Ludwig on one of his many visits to the front.

sized attack to the north against the Bois de Givenchy, which successfully regained the knoll at the northern end of Vimy Ridge from the French Tenth Army. 'The next day the French informed the British that the attack was serious and requested the relief of the two flank corps of the four holding the Tenth Army front. Later, the French Commander-in-Chief asked that, of strategic necessity, the Tenth Army should be relieved at once.'

'As an offensive against the Tenth Army front was considered unlikely, Haig decided to take over the whole of the front.' Between 2 and 14 March, the relief of Tenth Army was completed but not in the secrecy that had been intended. The British 46 Division went into the line on 9 March with advance parties going into the trenches wearing French helmets to disguise their arrival. However, the changeover was already known about by 7 March. On that day a 'French listening post reported that a German patrol had looked in and were heard to comment that the British had not yet arrived.'

'After Flanders the area was dry and bright. The relieving British troops found that the

Coastal guns set up in the gardens of a ruined house on the sea front.

May 1916 –
Shallow trenches
in the dunes on
the Belgian coast.

area from the Somme to Arras had seen practically no fighting since the line had settled down in 1914.'

'Whilst the British were moving in, *OHL* was anticipating its counterattack response to the Entente relief counterattacks; one favoured area was Arras but *6 Army* rejected this unless they were given more than the eight divisions promised. Falkenhayn rejected the proposal of a large-scale breakthrough attempt because there were insufficient troops available without seriously weakening the other fronts.'

'The Entente powers were in no position to launch a relief attack anywhere on the front and Verdun was using up the *OHL* reserve quicker than anticipated, so there would be no major second offensive, only a secondary one. Falkenhayn telegraphed *6 Army* on 4 April and asked whether they would be prepared to launch their offensive with four additional divisions and an increased number of heavy artillery batteries. Their reply was immediate: four divisions would allow them to take Loos and it would need three weeks of preparation before the attack. On 10 April, Falkenhayn ordered them to continue preparations for the Arras attack.' When the attack eventually materialised, with so many troops committed in Russia and at Verdun, there was no real possibility of building on the success achieved and the British were left alone.

'Verdun brought a number of new tools of war. Phosgene, a novel, colourless, asphyxiating gas, was first used at Verdun.' This was followed by gradual improvements in gas mask design. Large-scale use of portable flamethrowers was made in the tunnels of the Verdun forts. The first mass use of the Stahlhelm (steel helmet) was provided to troops in the massed attacks at Verdun. This was followed by experiments with steel arm shields and body armour. Ten-man Sturm battalions went into action and the German Army adopted a French rifle capable of firing grenades. All of these would soon find their way to the Flanders Front.

Something else that would find its way to other fronts was the change in attitude of the German soldier as a result of experience at Verdun. 'The German Army was heavily bled at Verdun: 48 divisions had gone through the "Meuse mill". Many of the troops lost faith in their leaders. For the first time discipline began to break down. Desertions

Bavarian Army motorised ambulance carrying wounded men to the field hospital.

mounted. "Police measures" were instituted to maintain discipline. The harmonious "spirit of 1914" was crushed.' According to Crown Prince Wilhelm, the "Meuse mill" ground up hearts as well as bodies. Ernst Toller, a Jewish war volunteer, felt that the Verdun experience, more so than the Flanders and Artois fighting, had changed attitudes to the war. 'The great patriotic feelings turned dull, the big words small; war becomes commonplace, service at the front day's work; heroes become victims, volunteers slaves; life is one hell, death is a mere trifle.'

The Verdun battles would continue until September and be joined by the Somme offensive later in the year. This would focus *OHL* for the remainder of the year. With fighting on the Eastern Front (Brusilov Offensive) and in Italy, there were insufficient men for any further major offensives.

Then on 27 August, Romania declared war on Austria-Hungary. The next day Germany declared war on Romania and within three weeks had assembled an invasion force of 200,000 men, half of them German. As a result of these internal and external pressures on the German Army throughout the year it would be a relatively quiet time for the Flanders Front, apart from attacks at St. Eloi, Observatory Ridge, Mount Sorrel and Hooge, to name but a few.

Law student Martin Müller had served in France from the beginning of the war but the start of 1916 found him in Belgium. Out of the line at Oostkamp, he wrote home on 19 March to tell his family how action-packed his time in Flanders had been so far. 'To-day the King (of Saxony) has awarded me the Cross of the Albert Order, 2nd Class, with Swords.' He was happy with this award, though it reminded him of a tragic experience that had occurred during a patrol he led against English positions on 28 January.

Müller had noticed that the enemy wire had been badly damaged and that all that was stopping an attack were a few isolated "Spanish Horsemen" (star-shaped frameworks wound round with barbed-wire, which could be thrown out on to no man's land from the trench). Collecting volunteers to investigate the wire, he realised that their leader, Fahnen-junker-Corporal Strauss, had never been out on patrol before, and so he led the patrol himself. They quickly crawled into no man's land with the bullets passing over-

Coastal guns set up in emplacements just behind the beach, near Westende.

head. Their progress slowed each time a star-shell went up but eventually they were close enough to hear coughing in the trench ahead of them.

As they watched, the British got out of their trench and headed for the wire Müller had come to inspect. They now had to find out whether the wire was being removed or repaired. Crawling closer, Müller could see new wire being stretched across iron pickets. As he motioned to the others to join him, one of the party was shot. Picking up their wounded comrade they withdrew under fire and ended up in an old water-logged trench that led to the English lines.

Realising that Tschoppe's wound was deep, Müller decided to use his greatcoat as a stretcher but found it too short, and the load too heavy, for two of them. Sending Strauss back for help he settled down to wait with the wounded man. After what seemed like hours Strauss, who had got lost, returned with another man to help bring Tschoppe in. Quickly, but gently laying Tschoppe on a groundsheet, they set off for their own lines,

An army cook feeding his chickens at Beverloo camp. This was a large training establishment through which recruits passed on their way to the front and where troops on rest were sent for further training.

A card to reassure those at home that everything was going well. An Unteroffizier in *238 Reserve Infantry Regiment* in *52 Reserve Division* sent this home in April 1916.

leaving their passenger at the aid post for transport to hospital. Müller himself was to die on 20 July while serving on the Somme.

Unable to retake The Bluff, the British chose to mount a retaliatory attack in the St. Eloi sector to remove a salient that penetrated their lines. The area had been mined and countermined throughout 1915 with the British firing thirteen mines against twenty German. Any advance would be hard going as the ground at St. Eloi was 'was waste of sticky mud broken by shell holes and mine craters of all sizes.' A surprise attack with no artillery was decided on for 27 April. Thirty seconds after the six mines had been fired, the assault would start. As the assaulting troops moved forward, the German artillery opened fire.

The British attack met with varying degrees of success; some prisoners were taken but some objectives could not be reached. Successful units were later hampered by the rain which filled the captured trenches. Later attempts to empty the trenches by pumping the water out failed because it was thick with mud which, once shovelled out, simply let the water drain back in.

On 6 April, battalions of *214* and *216 Reserve Regiments* made a successful assault and by 0600 hours the entire position lost on 27 March was regained. After days of fighting, the British had been unable to hold the ground. The vicious fighting at St. Eloi, by now no more than a heap of dusty rubble, had lasted 'until a sort of unspoken stalemate was reached.' The Official History states the fighting 'had imposed unheard-of misery upon the troops and both sides were glad to bring it to a close.' Casualties were heavy and several thousand men had been lost, 'including 300 Germans who had either been atomized or buried alive.' The official German losses were 107 dead, 267 wounded and 547 missing, of whom 201 were prisoners.

After the attacks at The Bluff and St. Eloi, 'the sector from south of Armentières to Boesinghe, beyond Ypres, had been comparatively quiet' apart from the ubiquitous shelling of British front and rear positions. The artillery had fallen into the habit of regular shelling that allowed the British to move in comparative safety. Unknown to the artillery, the shelling interfered with the British tunnelling preparations.

Mine warfare was quite normal in the salient, but plans were under way for a profound undertaking under Messines Ridge. After being appointed C-in-C of the BEF, Haig told

A dead aviator lies with his plane. Pilots were not issued with parachutes so, if they were shot down and could not land the plane they had to decide whether to stay with the plane or jump – both certain death.

General Plumer of his plans to attack at Ypres as soon as he could be ready. Any such attack would involve taking the Messines Ridge. In preparation for this, 'in early 1916 Plumer summoned the tunnelling companies and told them of a scheme of unprecedented magnitude. They were to dig twenty-one deep mine shafts beneath the ridge – some of them half a mile long – and fill them with an amount of explosive so far unheard of. The work involved in this was mind-boggling, thousands of miners tunnelling night and day, with tons of soil to be disposed of, and all off it to be done in utmost secrecy.' The plan was to blow Messines off the map with a million pounds of ammonal; a plan that was delayed by the battles of Verdun and then the Somme.

The size of the mining operations is clearly indicated by the British *Official History* that recorded April as a quiet month: 'there was very little mining activity...the Germans only blew seven mines, one of which on the 24th wrecked the deep offensive mine under la Petite Douve Farm.' It was quiet but preparations were being made for a gas attack. This

The ruins of Bixschoote church.

Soldiers of a field dressing station and a sanitation company pose for their photos in a Flanders village street.

was confirmed to the British by two deserters who confirmed the positioning of gas cylinders and by artillery shells exploding some of the cylinders. The truth of where the gas went depends upon the side reporting the gas cloud. In British reports, it fell on the German lines, but in the history of *Reserve Regiment 210*, a thirty foot high cloud, with flames in it, settled over and then sank into the British trenches.

Having been confirmed by two more deserters on 29 April, the attack was launched the next day, its purpose being to find and destroy mine galleries. Just after midnight, covered by the noise of rifle and machine gun fire, the hissing of the gas went virtually unnoticed. With the two front-lines in some places as close as forty yards, the first some of the British troops knew of the gas was the smell.

With the release came the artillery barrage, carefully placed on battery positions, observation posts, strongpoints and support trenches. In reply the British artillery opened fire. About five minutes after the gas release, the first troops approached the British wire

To help stave off boredom, each corps set up its own library where soldiers could read and borrow books. The books were donated by the public and packed at a central clearing house before being sent to the front.

but were driven back. When the gas stopped, further attempts were made to get into the British trenches, none of which were successful and by 0130 hours the artillery fire had ceased. To the British it appeared that the action was over but two further raids were made. Although covered by artillery fire and snipers, the raiders were turned back although one group did manage to lay a forty pound charge in a disused mine shaft. By 0430 hours the front was quiet.

Although the British mining work was carried out as secretly as possible, the German Mineure (miners) were convinced that Wytschaete-Bogen (Wytschaete Ridge) was of special interest to the British miners. While the Somme battles were being fought, Lt. Colonel Füsslein's men were probing under the ridge to establish the extent of the British effort. Their first success was in August when they found a tunnel under Petit Douve Farm. It was a pyrrhic victory as the British blew a heavy charge (camouflet) when the German miners were removing the explosive.

Shortly after this, the Mineure exploded a charge equivalent to 6,000 lbs of ammonal near the British main tunnel. It wrecked the main tunnel and killed four of the British soldiers working in it. Now aware that something big was happening, but not knowing what, the Mineure were helped by the defection of a Canadian tunneller. He provided Füsslein with the 'location of the mineshafts for Trench 122 and Factory Farm. The British front line opposite was soon heavily shelled and a week later, a large raid was carried out.'

Now convinced this activity would be followed by a British attack at some point, Füsslein requested further men. Although given three further companies, it was still insufficient. His superiors refused to take the mining war seriously – with serious consequences a year later. The tables were turning in favour of the Allies. In 1916 the British blew 750 mines to the Germans' 696.

All mining was difficult and dangerous work, but more so on the German side. Holding the higher ground meant that they had to tunnel deeper and further. Successful shafts, sunk through the shifting geology of running sand, into the clay beneath, were mainly of concrete and steel. On top of the constructional difficulties there was also the problem

The Grand Duke of Hesse inspecting his troops in August 1916.

of getting materials to the front. Oberstleutnant Füsslein described the difficulties. 'Iron rings, metal rods, sand, cement, aggregate and all our equipment had to be brought forward first on rail trucks, then by narrow-gauge railway behind the lines, and then finally manhandled into position through muddy, cratered trenches under enemy fire' that destroyed the workings and killed the miners. Although specialist troops, they had a further problem: they were also used as infantrymen.

The Entente had not been inactive and in early April, *Second Army* reported that the British 'were making preparations for a large-scale attack; they were digging jumping-off trenches and were ranging their artillery.' The preparations were 'the beginnings of the long-planned battle of the Somme.' Throughout the year, the focus on both sides would be Verdun and the Somme. Flanders would become a quieter front: an area where troops could be sent to rest, recover and reorganise. Looking at the divisions that served in Flanders during the year, it is clear that many of them only spent a short period in the area before being returned to the front they had been sent from. *58 Division* was a typical example. It had been heavily engaged during the Somme battle and on 19 September was placed in a quiet sector on the Yser Front until 23 October, when it returned to the Somme.

In Flanders, quiet continued to be a relative term. Corps orders of 20 May concerned a future attack on Mount Sorrel – Tor Top ridge. The attack was to be carried out by the divisions in the line, after six weeks of secret preparations. To assist in reducing the fortifications, heavy artillery had been borrowed from other corps as well as light, medium and heavy trench mortars. On the night of 1/2 June, the assault troops moved into the trenches to await the order to attack.

The trenches at Messines in the summer of 1916. An officer and soldier of *46 Reserve Division* at a concealed periscope bay.

The attack was to be limited to a total advance of 500 yards. 'At seven minutes past one o'clock on the afternoon of the 2nd June, the German *XIII.(Württemberg) Corps,* with some assistance from the corps on its flanks, after lengthy and careful preparation, assaulted the sector of the front of the Canadian Corps which lay between Hill 60 and Hooge, where no man's land averaged less than one hundred and fifty yards wide.'

Preceded by a terrific bombardment and the explosion of three mines, the successful assault captured Observatory Ridge near Mount Sorrel (actually a hill). This was the last portion of the crest of Ypres Ridge to be taken from the British. Not only was the intention to take the ridge with its excellent views of the British back areas, in an attempt

A large calibre British naval shell explodes harmlessly on the beach somewhere on the Belgian coast.

to make the British withdraw towards Ypres, only two miles away, but it also aimed at pulling British troops away from the Somme.

Prior to the attack, the artillery had ranged the area but was silent from 2000 hours on 1 June until 0300 hours in order not to interfere with the men cutting passages in their own and the British wire. Then the guns resumed their normal activity until about 0830 hours when the intensity increased. At 1230 hours the bombardment quickened and trench mortars joined in. An observer in *Infantry Regiment 120* described the scene. 'The whole enemy position was a cloud of dust and dirt, into which timber, tree trunks, weapons and equipment were continuously hurled up, and occasionally human bodies.' Shell fire obliterated trenches, shelters, wire, and all the defences.

After heavy hand-to-hand, grenade and bayonet fighting, the ridge was taken. It was held for eleven days until it was retaken by the Canadians. By the end of the battle both sides were back in their original positions. The cost of the brief occupation had been expensive: 109 officers killed, wounded or missing and 5,656 other ranks killed, wounded or missing. Canadian losses had been even heavier: 387 officers and 8,043 other ranks killed, wounded or missing.

The main street of Bixschoote in 1916. Little is still habitable.

The coastal trenches during the winter of 1916.

On the night of 16/17 June, gas was released west of Messines where no man's land was between 400 and 600 yards wide. Although the wind was favourable and the gas cloud dense, the light wind gave the British time to get their helmets on. Before the assault had started, the wind changed direction and the British artillery put down an effective barrage. The few men who tried to leave their trench soon returned.

The raiding and shelling continued but no major assaults occurred for the rest of the year. Although comparatively quiet on the ground, there was much aerial and naval activity with the British bombing airfields and Zeppelin sheds and the Germans bombing the rear positions and Ypres.

'Even though the intentions of the Entente on the Somme were clearly known, *6 Army* was holding a shorter line than *2 Army* on the Somme, with seventeen and a half divisions and large amounts of heavy artillery. Falkenhayn intended to launch his counteroffensive at Arras after the British had exhausted themselves on the Somme. He assumed that the

A grave marker at Bixschoote made of spent cases, unexploded shells and empty shrapnel shells.

A card sent home by a soldier in *117 Division* in October 1916. He is wearing older style ammunition pouches and is probably a Landwehr soldier.

line at Arras would be held by second-rate and inexperienced divisions that would provide less resistance, allowing any local breakthrough to be turned into a strategic success. To ensure success *OHL* kept some of its best divisions deployed near or with *6 Army*. With *2 Army* reinforced to take the Entente offensive and continued pressure on the French at Verdun, 'forces for the counterstroke had been mustered' and their deployment begun.' Once again Flanders would be left out of the operation, especially as all but one of the reserve divisions were now fighting in Russia or on the Somme. There were no troops left to mount a further offensive.

The failure of Falkenhayn's strategy for 1916 weakened his support within the army. As the situation worsened over the summer, calls for a restriction of his authority, or even his dismissal, became more vocal. By August, even his closest supporters had turned against him. With no support within the army or government, the Kaiser, against his better judgment, was forced to replace him with Hindenburg and Ludendorff. On 29 September they took over direction of Germany's strategic effort, ending the Verdun offensive on 2 September to refocus German efforts.

They decided to end what they saw as a primitive 'form of trench warfare in favour of a more sophisticated system of defences along the Western Front. Specifically they opted to straighten out a 20-mile bulge along a 65-mile front in *Army Group Crown Prince Rupprecht's* sector and in the process create a great defensive arc along the line Lens-Noyon-Reims.' A withdrawal to this Siegfried Stellung would both reduce the length of the front line and also increase the number of troops available as reserves. It was an obvious choice but *OHL* did not sanction the withdrawal.

Future activity would be based on knowledge learned during the year. German defensive positions were not to be held at all costs, fewer men were to be in the front-line, and the linear trench system, roughly one mile in depth, was replaced by a killing zone between six and eight miles in depth. Concrete bunkers housed machine guns and new tactics were adopted for this defence in depth.

'Convinced that the Allies would mount major offensives in the spring of 1917 and deeply shaken by the experience at the Somme, the Supreme Command debated the best

A card sent by a soldier in *24 Reserve Division* that clearly shows the conditions during the winter of 1915–16.

course of action for 1917.' *First, Sixth* and *Seventh Armies* and *Crown Prince Rupprecht's Army Group* had taken the brunt of the Somme fighting and were classed as exhausted and used up. Crown Prince Wilhelm's *Fifth Army* had been bled to death at Verdun.

General von Kohl believed that the German losses hit harder than did those of the Allies. Each year it was becoming more difficult to replace the losses. The commander of *27 Infantry Division,* General-Leutnant von Moser, ably summed up the position of the German Army at the end of 1916: 'The formations which were deployed during the Battle of the Somme were very worn down physically and their nerves were badly affected. The huge gaps torn in the ranks could only be filled out by returning wounded, nineteen-year-olds who were too young, or by combing out from civilian occupations, men who, to a large extent, due to their physical condition or mental attitude, could not be regarded as fully effective troops.'

As well as better training for officers and the artillery, Ludendorff, impressed by the work of the Sturmbataillons at Verdun and the Somme 'intensified their creation and training. By November the new "workers of war" had been outfitted with special vests to carry hand-grenades, gas masks, bread sacks, field flasks, daggers, and light machine guns.' A typical storm battalion led by a captain with four lieutenants carried a considerable sized arsenal: '24 light machine guns, 8 trench mortars, 8 light mortars, 8 flamethrowers, 4 light artillery pieces, heavy machine guns, and a signal horn.'

An increase in manpower was essential. Reserve formations had been shown to be critical. 'On 2 September Ludendorff demanded eight new divisions, including five for the Western Front. The Prussian War Ministry agreed at once to release 72,000 men mustered fit for garrison duty and promised another 57,000 in the near future.' The early call-up of the 1916 class, returning wounded and the newly released men provided the army with 1.3 million reserves, allowing the creation of thirteen new infantry divisions in the winter of 1916/1917.

At the same time as Ludendorff managed to increase the size of the army, it became essential to increase the production of war material. As a result, some men had to be returned temporarily to the Home Front. In the winter of 1916-17 this amounted to

A photo taken near the Belgian border in late 1916. It clearly shows the desolation and conditions in which the men lived and fought. The narrow gauge railway line was used to bring supplies up as close as possible to the front.

125,000 men who would be returned to the army only when they could be spared.

An obvious answer to the manpower shortage was the conscription of unemployed Belgians in the occupied zone. Additional manpower was provided by Poland and the other occupied countries. Further assistance was provided unintentionally by the huge numbers of POWs taken on the Eastern Front. To Ludendorff they were of the utmost importance in all fields of war activity; they held the German economic structure together.

The battles of Verdun and the Somme had caused a very heavy wastage of artillery, not just through Allied shelling but also through excessive use. Production increased to replace and provide new guns to increase their effectiveness. The production of long-range artillery to harass the Allied rear areas was increased as was the number of 'super heavies', those requiring railway mountings. Increased Model 06 field gun and armour-piercing bullet production was seen as the answer to the British tanks. Ammunition supply

The Christmas celebrations 1916 at Knocke-sur-Mer.

and fuse construction were simplified, shrapnel was abandoned, smoke shells were manufactured and gas shell production increased.

Ludendorff knew that the Allies had a greater production capacity than Germany; he was also aware of the advantage this gave them. This was especially true of transport. Lorries were desperately needed to replace the worn-out horses, for which there were too few replacements, but industry could only produce lorries in numbers so small that they could be used for troop movements only in emergencies. The Allies on the other hand had so many that they could be used just to take troops back and forth to their billets. While the number of Allied tanks grew, there was insufficient industrial capacity to produce German tanks. In all ways the Allies were outstripping German industry. It had become a matériel war.

In Flanders, rain had turned the low-lying regions 'into slime and the men found little comfort in the shell craters that they used as dug-outs.' On the Somme, the men were exhausted and used up. The prospect of renewed Allied attacks supported by hundreds of tanks left little room for

A Christmas postcard sent by a member of an airforce squadron.

Christmas 1916, just behind the lines.

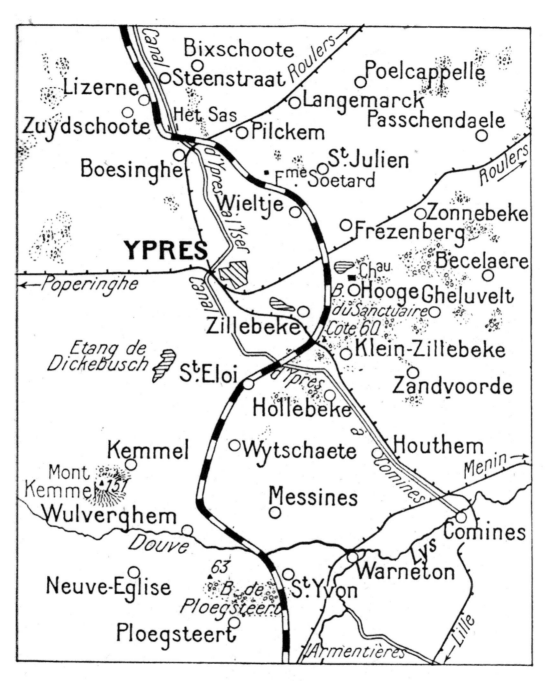

THE FRONT LINE FROM JUNE 1915 TO JUNE 1917.

optimism. Crown Prince Rupprecht repeatedly requested permission to withdraw to new defensive positions. A strategic withdrawal over a three month period would release eleven divisions and shorten the front. However, 'at the end of 1916 the Siegfried Stellung was only to be regarded as a "factor of safety" and there was no intention of voluntarily retiring to it.'

Winter 1916 was the third and as yet the worst of the war. 'It froze the feet and souls of the men on both sides of the wire: sentinels of their respective front lines, existing in a surreal, troglodyte world. The winter of 1916/17 was the coldest for more than 30 years…it was bleak, iron-hard and enduring. As the season took hold it seemed as though it, like the war, would be endless.'

An open-air concert for anyone who happens to be near. Military bands often gave concerts in public places to help improve relationships with the civilian population.

Base hospital staff in Namur. After initial treatment, wounded soldiers were sent to a field and then base hospital like this one. Those that were more seriously wounded could hope to be sent home to recover.

Out of the line on rest, men continued to train and learn new skills. Gas mask drill was essential for survival in the trenches.

Dugout built under the ruins of a large building in Dixmude.

The Iron Hindenburg, next to the Victory Column in the Köningsplatz, designed by Georg Marschall and inaugurated on 4 September 1915; Princess August Wilhelm drove the first nail into Hindenburg's name on the plinth. 1.15 million marks were raised. People donated a sum to charity for the right to hammer a nail into the wooden statue.

Food production was an essential part of the war effort. During crucial periods, troops were provided to help out in any way they could.

An artist's card showing a hand grenade fight.

Hindenburg and his staff on the Eastern Front, just before he was transferred to take over the running of the Western Front. After his victories in Russia, he had become a national hero who was expected to always win.

Camouflage was always important in siting artillery. Here a ruined coastal house is used to disguise a sea-facing gun.

Officers of *III Battalion 123 Grenadier Regiment* relaxing in their quarters. Allied intelligence rated them as very good troops.

Troops inspecting newly-captured English foxholes in a wood near Ypres.

Jakob Spirkl, an innkeeper in Rothenwörth, died in a Munich hospital on 30 January. He had been serving in Flanders when he was wounded.

A grave marker in Poelkapelle churchyard for the dead of *Infantry Regiment 83*.

King Albert of Belgium was keen to keep up morale in the free Belgian zone. Here he is visiting positions near Dixmude.

POWs pose with their guards before entraining for a camp in Germany. The card was sent by a soldier in *Grenadier Regiment 123,* a unit in *27 Infantry Division*, and shows Canadian troops captured by the division during the assault on Observatory Ridge in the Cillebeke sector.

There was little to do when the daily chores were completed. Many a unit had its talented amateur artist who would draw cards for the men to send home. This is of an unknown Landwehr soldier.

From the other side: the machine gun section of Belgian Line Infantry Regiment 13 pose with their M1895 Colt-Browning machine gun.

Sea soldiers bringing home the bacon.

Marines inspecting a newly-captured British trench.

The threat of gas was constant even on the coast. Here marines practise crawling while wearing gas masks.

Officers and men of *I Machine Gun Company of III Battalion Grenadier Regiment 123 of 27 (Württemberg) Division* at rest somewhere behind the Sanctuary Wood positions.

A joke for the scrapbook. 'My friends after a heavy battle'. Carrying home the pig for dinner.

Naval aviators preparing to take off on their next sortie. These aircraft bombed Allied camps, airfields and towns to the south and as far away as Dover.

Patriotic art card extolling the *Naval Corps* in Flanders. 'Always at their post'.

Officers and ratings inspecting the damage caused by a large calibre shell to the sand dunes.

New recruits for the sea soldiers who manned the coastal defences of Belgium.

Artillery officers stretching their legs on Poelcapelle station, while the men stay with their equipment.

Four infantrymen see the New Year in by having their photo taken for the folk back home.

A view of no man's land from the German trenches somewhere near Ypres, showing the utter desolation.

At rest behind the front. The comparative luxury of officers' quarters.

With most of the civilian population having left Ostend, German naval and military personnel were the main source of income for those that had stayed.

A postcard printed in Hamburg for sale to the troops in Flanders. A street scene in Passchendaele.

Diorama of the Ypres front.

m Ypern" I.

traat, Dickebusch u. Vlamertinghe, gem. Herbst 1916-

m Ypern" II

ële, Ypern u. St. Jean, gem. Herbst 1916-

(35) **Straße in Passchendaele** Von den Engländern zerschossen

A street in Passchendaele after a British artillery bombardment. A card sent by Gefreiter Klages, serving with *18 Reserve Division* north of Ypres.

Narrow-gauge railways could be built almost anywhere to allow the rapid movement of stores and people as close to the front as possible.

A Belgian postcard showing the inundations in front of Pervyse station that stopped any attacks after 1914.

As with all plane crashes, this shot down Airco DH2 was a 'tourist draw'.

The Porte de Lille in the battlements in Ypres. Athough it was not held by the German Army, cards of Ypres were often sent home by soldiers serving in the area. This was sent to Mittelfranken in Bavaria by a soldier serving in *Bavarian Reserve Infantry Regiment 20,* a unit in *6 Bavarian Reserve Division.*

Death by shell fire was random. The picture shows two almost simultaneous explosions in a field behind the line.

A rear echelon warehouse. Most of the shelves contain little or nothing.

Sea soldier 1914-16. A hand drawn card of the last positions on the Belgian coast.

The devastation at Sanctuary Wood after the fighting there during 1916.

A Sanitary unit at rest – the Nolte Family in Flanders 1914-1916; sanitary units dealt with casualties and general health matters.

The headquarters of a Sanitation company, hidden in a wood somewhere in Belgium.

Seesoldaten im Schützengraben.

Sea soldiers, now in field-grey uniforms man their trenches in the dunes.

Soldiers' quarters in Poelcapelle.

Soldiers' quarters in Poelcapelle being inspected.

Staden. — Yperstraat.

Ypres Street in Staden, before the war.

Staff officers inspecting the damage in a Flanders village caused by a British heavy mortar.

German barbarians playing cards at their billets during the summer of 1916 in Flanders.

Landwehr soldiers were the oldest troops in the army and because of this they were the butt of many jokes about their abilities.

A well behind the front propaganda photograph, to illustrate what conditions were like at the front line. The enemy must be a considerable distance away as one soldier is showing his head above the trench structure – inviting sniper attention.

A sanitised view of the trenches with perfect walls and almost spotless duckboards.

A carefully concealed mine entrance in a front line trench. Mine warfare was common in the Ypres sector and raids were regularly carried out to find and blow such entrances.

There were miles of trenches in the dunes. The instability of the sand made their maintenance very difficult for the troops.

A card sent by a soldier in 7 *Bavarian Infantry Regiment*, of 5 *Bavarian Infantry Division*. It clearly shows the threat to British shipping. The card is titled 'England's blockade – our U-boats at work.'

A card sold to raise funds for a naval charity. It is titled 'U-boat attack'.

Two unexploded naval shells (305 mm and 85 mm) fired at targets on the Belgian coast. Amusingly the card was sent by a member of the munitions column of a division in Flanders.

Vinzenz Mangler, a soldier in *Bavarian Infantry Regiment 20*, died in *field hospital 47* on 31 May 1916 after being wounded in Flanders.

A close-up of the shell damage sustained by Zonnebeke village

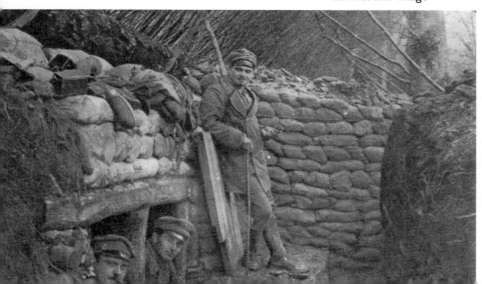

A well-constructed trench in West Flanders, using sandbags for stability and having a partial cover to deter grenades and visitors.

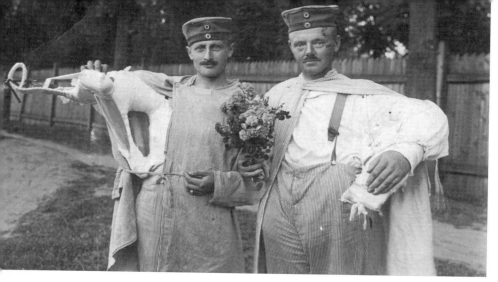

Two wounded soldiers proudly show off their bandages for their families at home and show that they are in reasonably good health.

The ruins of Ypres by the mid-point of the war.

The ruins of Zanvoorde after British shelling.

Chronology of the Flanders Front – 1915

THE FIRST GERMAN POISON-GAS ATTACK.
(*April 24, 1915.*)

'The Friedrichshafen FF.33 was a German single-engined amphibious reconnaissance biplane designed by Flugzeugbau Friedrichshafen in 1914.' It carried a pilot and observer/gunner with an armament of 1 flexible mount 7.92 mm Parabellum MG14 in rear cockpit and 8 × 26.4 lb (12 kg) bombs. Many flew from Belgian bases as bombers and in this case as a rescue plane, saving an enemy flier in the North Sea.

'The initial production version was powered by a Mercedes D.II engine inline water-cooled engine, six examples of this variant were built. The basic design was refined and improved. The FF.33e main production reconnaissance variant was powered by a Benz B.III inline engine. This version had longer twin floats, and the under tail central float was eliminated. A radio transmitter replaced its armament; approximately 180 examples of the FF.33e variant were built.'

1915

1 January	Artillery duels at Nieuport and Zonnebeke. First of twenty five A1 type small torpedo boats commissioned for Flanders coastal operations.
2 January	Heavy rain hampers any offensive action on both sides.
4 January	French attack near Nieuport not held.
16 January	Under French artillery fire, troops retire from coastal dunes near Nieuport.
19 January	Operations impeded by snow storm.
22 January	RNAS drop twenty seven bombs on Zeebrugge U-boat base
23 January	Small loss to enemy attacks near Nieuport.
25 January	Attacks on British positions at Givenchy, and on French positions near Ypres repulsed.
28 January	Great Dune lost to enemy attack.

A comrade contemplates the grave of Leutnant H Beck who died on 25 January 1915. The card was sent by a gunner serving in *4 Battery Reserve Artillery Regiment 7*.

11 February	Three RNAS aircraft bomb Zeebrugge and Ostend U-boat bases and coastal batteries. French diversionary raid on Ghistelles airfield.
1 February	Trenches near Cuinchy stormed by British.
20 February	Small section of forward trench near Ypres captured.
1 March	Fifteen Indian soldiers desert; eventually returned to the North-west Frontier.
4 March	Belgian troops shoot down naval airship L8 en route to London.
5 March	Army airship L233 shot down by anti-aircraft fire, and crashes near Ostend.
7 March	Six RNAS aircraft bomb Ostend.
8 March	Belgian positions near Dixmude attacked.
14 March	Troops pushed back by Belgian attack near Dixmude.
23 March	Belgian troops land on the east bank of the River Yser.
24 March	Two RNAS aircraft bomb coastal U-boat assembly yards at Hoboken, Antwerp.
29 March	Flanders U-boat flotilla activated with 127 ton coastal UB boats and 168 ton UC minelayers. U-boats assembled at Antwerp and towed to Bruges-Zeebrugge via canals.
30 March	POWs provide enemy with details of plans to use asphyxiating gas from cylinders near Zillebeke.

A concrete headquarters building. As the area is clean, this is obviously some way from the front. One soldier is holding a gas cylinder, others are relaxing. All wear jackets with Saxon cuffs (two buttons). The bunker was built in 1915 and is inscribed with the same words as on a soldier's belt buckle: 'Gott mit uns'. The bunker is multi-purpose: headquarters, first aid post, telephone post and bomb shelter for all ranks.

1 April	Cloister Hoek occupied. Hoboken U-boat assembly yards bombed by RNAS.
4 April	General Below takes over *Second Army* after General Bülow is placed on retired list after suffering a stroke.
5 April	Belgian attack at Driegrachten repulsed.
8 April	Gas attack postponed due to poor weather.
9 April	French sink rafts carrying assault troops attacking St. Jacques Capelle south of Dixmude.
12 April	Unsuccessful attack on enemy positions near Dixmude.
13 April	Army airship L235 damaged by anti-aircraft fire while bombing Poperinghe, and wrecked in forced landing near Ypres.
14 April	Private Jäger from *234 Reserve Infantry Regiment*, captured near Langemarck, provides enemy with details of the planned gas attack, but is not believed.
17 April	After detonating three mines, the British take and hold Hill 60 against counter-attacks.
19 April	Further fighting at Hill 60.
20 April	Test firing of gas shells on British positions at Hill 60. Heavy shelling of Ypres called a 'Hate Shoot' by the British, causes damage, kills civilians and forces many to leave the town.

A French trench in front of Ypres, captured on 23 April 1915. The card was sent by a soldier serving with *Infantry Regiment 91*, a unit in *19 Infantry Division*, to his friend serving in *1 Garde Reserve Division* in Flanders. At the time, the sender was serving on the Aisne in France.

22 April	Second Battle of Ypres starts with attacks on Gravenstafel Ridge. Big Berthas shell Ypres. *Fourth Army* releases first gas attack on the Western Front at 1700 hours near Langemarck. The 3¾ mile front is lined with 4000 chlorine gas cylinders that release 168 tons of the gas in five minutes over the French Algerian and Canadian divisions in the area. Wearing respirators, two divisions 'mop up' on Pilckem Ridge, taking about 2000 POWs and 51 guns. Gas causes Algerian troops to flee across the canal, leaving a gap in their lines. After fierce fighting, Canadian Wood, west of St. Julien, is taken.
23 April	Second gas attack. Allied counter-attack collapses, resulting in the loss of Langemarck, Steenstraate Bridge and positions south of Lizerne.
24 April	Release of gas on Allied positions at St. Julien allows their capture, but west of Lizerne the Franco-Belgian positions are not taken. Canadian attacks on Lizerne force troops back.
26 April	Heavy fighting around Ypres, but gas helps contain Allied advance. Franco-Belgian positions south of Dixmude attacked with gas. Courtrai station bombed. Ghent area bombed by RFC in an attempt to disrupt troop movements to Ypres. Stations and trains on the Staden-Cortemarck-Roulers line attacked by RFC.
27 April	Around Ypres, troops pushed back by Allied attacks, with French retaking Lizerne.
28 April	Allied positions in Dunkirk shelled by guns in Dixmude.
29 April	Three boat-bridges across the Yser destroyed by Belgian artillery.
30 April	French attack achieves very limited success.
1 May	No progress made by attack on Allied positions at Hill 60 even though gas is used. French counter-attack fails and British start to pull back to new defensive line.
2 May	Attacks on Allied positions in the area of St. Julien, using gas, are repulsed.

4 May	British have withdrawn to a line from Mouse-trap Farm – Frezenberg Ridge – Hill 60. Troops between Het Sas and Lizerne fail to hold French attack.
5 May	British positions on Hill 60 taken after a heavy gas attack.
6 May	Heavy fighting results in the loss of some trenches on Hill 60 to British.
8 May	Frezenberg Ridge taken after heavy bombardment starting at 0530 hours, but after heavy fighting the advance is only about a kilometre.
9 May	British attack on Aubers Ridge in French Flanders results in heavy casualties but, further north, east of Ypres, Wieltje is successfully recaptured.
10 May	British attack on Aubers Ridge continues with heavy casualties for the attackers.
11 May	Two battalions accidentally gassed during bombardment of enemy positions on the Ypres-Menin Road.

The château at Polderhoek showing the effect of British and French artillery.

May 1915. A mixed group of Naval and Army personnel pose for the camera on the Flanders coast.

Hôtel Dieu, a temporary POW camp for the wounded. A postcard printed in Brussels and sent by a soldier serving in *Field Artillery Regiment 63*.

No 15 - Hôtel-Dieu.

13 May	Heavy bombardment of Ypres area; Frezenberg Ridge fighting ends.
14 May	Troops in Het Sas and Steenstraate unable to hold back Franco-Belgian attack.
15 May	French take Het Sas and regain east bank of canal.
20 May	First British observation balloon used near Poperinghe behind Ypres.
24 May	After heavy fighting on Bellewaarde Ridge, four divisions capture Mouse-trap Farm but lose other gains, despite early morning 4 ½ mile – wide gas cloud over British positions.
27 May	*Fourth Army* unable to mount any further attacks until ammunition replenished.
29 May	First UC type mine laying boat patrol from Zeebrugge by UC11.
30 May	Allied positions at Hooge attacked.

A card from Belgium to Dresden. Ernst Fritsche, serving with 53 Reserve Infantry Division, sends *Whitsuntide* greetings to family friends. Even though there was a war on, the Christian festivals still had significance.

FRÖHLICHE PFINGSTEN

SENDET AUS DEM FELDE

3 June	Ypres shelled.
16 June	British attack north of Hooge, after making some ground towards Bellewaarde Farm, is held with the ridge still in the hands of the defenders.
1 July	*Guards Cavalry Division* leaves Flanders for Poland.
3 July	Raid on Allied advanced trenches on Verlorenhoek Road near Ypres.
6 July	Trenches between Boesinghe and Ypres stormed by British troops.
14 July	Attack on Belgian positions along the Yser Canal repulsed.
19 July	Redoubt at Hooge lost after British mine explodes.
30 July	British positions on the Menin Road near Hooge attacked with flamethrowers and stormed by *126 Infantry Regiment* of *53 Reserve Division*.
1 August	British counter-attack at Hooge.
9 August	British recapture trenches at Hooge lost on 30 July and make further gains to the north and west.
15 August	Shelling on the Yser sector.
23 August	Dover Patrol monitors shell Knocke and Zeebrugge.
26 August	U-boat damaged near Ostend by RFC bombs.
7 September	Ostend bombarded by Dover Patrol and French ships using air-spotting. Monitor Lord Clive damaged by shells from the new *Tirpitz Battery* of four eleven inch guns.
10 September	Enemy positions at Rams-capelle and Skenstraate shelled.
13 September	Pilot and Secret Agent, both wounded, captured near Courtrai after their plane crashes during an attempt to infiltrate the agent into Belgium.
14 September	Canadian troops arrive on Ypres front and take over positions at Kemmel.
18 September	Positions on the Belgian coast shelled by French guns and the Royal Navy.
19 September	Ostend bombarded from sea.
25 September	Enemy feint attacks on the Yser near the Ypres-Comines Canal. Belgian coast bombarded from sea. Tirpitz battery bombed by the RNAS.

A fund-raising card for the U boat service. The Flanders ports were home to many such craft; a threat to the Royal Navy's domination of the North Sea.

A captured British Airco DH 1 on display in Flanders.

26 September	Belgian coast bombarded from sea.
27 September	Belgian coast bombarded from sea.
29 September	British trenches at Hooge taken but lost later in the day.
30 September	Belgian coast bombarded from sea.
1 October	Lombaertzyde, Middelkerke and Zeebrugge shelled.
2 October	Ypres heavily shelled.
3 October	Zeebrugge shelled.
10 October	Indian Corps leaves the Salient.
13 October	Artillery batteries silenced by very effective enemy artillery bombardments.
15 October	Little activity over the past week, except for artillery exchanges, due to the heavy rain.
17 October	Zeebrugge shelled.
18 October	Trenches southwest of Messines raided by Canadians.
5 December	Communication trenches near Het Sas shelled by French artillery.
7 December	Flooded trenches on the Yser abandoned.
10 December	Over 3000 shells fired on enemy positions in the salient.
19 December	Phosgene gas, ten times as toxic as Chlorine, is used on the British at Pilckem-Wieltje, north of Ypres, resulting in heavy casualties but not achieving the desired effect of producing a panic.

Johann Eichinger a twenty-eight year soldier from Holzhäuser who was killed in Flanders on 23 September 1915.

Relaxing on the wooden bridge across a section of the Yser in German hands, during the autumn of 1915.

20 December	Ypres shelled.
25 December	Generally quiet along the front with intermittent minor artillery duels.
28 December	Artillery activity in the Ypres area.
31 December	Successful attack on enemy positions near Hulluch.

Weihnachten 1915

Christmas 1915 in an officers' mess.

Chronology of the Flanders Front 1916

1916

6 January	Coastal batteries shelled by five Royal Navy monitors.
15 January	Royal Navy monitors shell Westeinde.
24 January	Diversionary attack on Nieuport to aid attacks on French positions near Arras.
27 January	Royal Navy monitors shell Westeinde.
12 February	Further diversionary attacks on enemy positions near Steenstraate, Boesinghe and Wissenbuch.
14 February	600 yards of enemy trenches taken north of the Ypres Canal, south of the Ypres-Comines railway and near St. Eloi.

The heavy reliance on horse drawn transport kept blacksmiths very busy.

Gefr. Sumpf.   Gefr. Rüßer   Gefr. Rudloff. Ers. Res. Wittke. Kan. Henschel.
astw. „Zum strammen Hund)   Gefr. Adam.

A named group of Landwehr soldiers enjoying coffee on Sunday 30 April 1916 in Flanders.

20 February	Three attempts to cross the Yser Canal near Boesinghe unsuccessful.
1 March	Flanders U-boat Flotilla now has twenty boats.
2 March	Positions taken on 14 February north of Ypres-Comines Canal, lost to British attack.
20 March	Four and a half tons of bombs dropped on Zeebrugge float plane base by Belgian, British and French planes.
27 March	1st and 2nd line trenches on a 600 yard front lost to British attack at St. Eloi craters south of Ypres.
3 April	Successful British attacks at St. Eloi.
6 April	After retaking crater at St. Eloi, positions lost to British counterattack.
10 April	RFC aircraft shot down at height of 8000 feet by anti-aircraft fire near Ypres.
12 April	British positions on Ypres-Pilckem Road attacked.
19 April	British positions at St. Eloi on Ypres-Langemarck Road taken, but lost later in the day to a British counterattack.
23 April	Mariakerke airfield, west of Ostend, bombed by RNAS.
24 April	British vessels laying a coastal barrage of mines and nets off the Flanders coast attacked by seaplanes, shore guns and three destroyers, damaging four ships. Mariakerke airfield, west of Ostend, bombed for the second time by RNAS.
30 April	British artillery stops gas attack on Messines Ridge.
1 May	Positions east of Ypres lost.
5 May	Mariakerke airfield bombed by the RNAS during the night of 5/6 May.
16 May	Destroyers patrolling off Belgian coast attacked by Royal Navy Dover Patrol.
19 May	Ghistelles airfield bombed. Dunkirk bombed during day and night. The 372 bombs dropped cause 121 casualties. Two of the attacking aircraft shot down by the RNAS.
21 May	Mariakerke airfield attacked for the fourth time in a month.

North African troops taken prisoner in early 1916. A card sent by a soldier in *Garde Reserve Regiment 2,* in *I Garde Reserve Division,* serving in the Wytschaete-Messines sector.

27 May	UC3 hits mine and sinks off Zeebrugge.
28 May	*Sixth Army* reinforced with three divisions in readiness for possible attack by British before Somme offensive.
2 June	Major attack on British positions between Hooge and Ypres-Roulers railway creates bulge in the line 700 yards deep and 3000 yards wide, killing one general and wounding another who is taken prisoner.
3 June	Troops unable to contain Canadian counterattack and trenches lost.
4 June	Three destroyers engage British destroyers north of Zeebrugge.
6 June	Attack at Hooge successful and some gains made.
13 June	Zillebeke positions lost to a Canadian attack.
8 July	Tirpitz battery shelled.
2 August	Zeppelin sheds in Brussels, Courtrai station and St. Denis Westrem airfield bombed.
I September	Three Flanders based UB-type U-boats sink over thirty ships in a week.
2 September	Ghistelles and St. Denis Westrem airfields bombed respectively by seventeen and eighteen RNAS aircraft. Brussels Zeppelin sheds attacked.
8 September	Coast between Middlekerke and Westende shelled by Royal Navy

General von Falkenhayn commanded the army until replaced by Hindenburg and Ludendorff in September 1916.

A British aircraft shot down intact is being inspected by officers from a nearby airfield.

	monitors.
9 September	Ghistelles airfield bombed.
21 September	Convoy straggler, SS Colchester, captured and taken into Zeebrugge.
23 September	Ghistelles airfield bombed.
27 September	Brussels Zeppelin sheds attacked.
26 October	Twenty six destroyers from Zeebrugge, led by Captain Michelson, raid the Dover Straits over the night of 26/27 October.
28 October	Zeebrugge bombed; little damage but torpedo boats lie up at Bruges.
9 November	RNAS seaplanes bomb Ostend docks and Zeebrugge.
10 November	Ostend raided by RNAS bombers.
12 November	Ostend raided by RNAS bombers.
15 November	RNAS seaplanes bomb Ostend docks and Zeebrugge.
17 November	RNAS seaplanes bomb Ostend docks and Zeebrugge.

Christmas in the cookhouse is obviouslu more pleasurable than being in the trenches. A card to wish those at home Warm Christmas greetings from Flanders.

22 November	Zeebrugge bombed.
23 November	Thirteen Zeebrugge destroyers damage one British Dover barrage drifter.
26 November	*OHL* issues instruction on role of Siegfried Stellung: 'Just as in times of peace, we build fortresses, so we are now building rearward defences. Just as we have kept clear of our fortresses, so we shall keep at a distance from these rearward defences'.
6 December	Berlin casualty office ceases to publish regular Verlustliste (casualty lists) with details of name, regiment and other particulars. The new lists were to be in alphabetical order with no further information.
12 December	Peace proposal made to the Allies.
14 December	Both sides make heavy raids near Ypres.

Histories of the Divisions that fought in Flanders

Military history is mostly written about the movement of units, some large, some small, with personal experience added where relevant, but rarely dealing with the history and origin of the troops involved.

Unlike the British Army, apart from the initially war-raised service battalions and the Territorial units, the German Army was rigidly territorially based so that divisions had a regional flavour until later in the war; even then every effort was made to maintain this by using men from the Landwehr and Landsturm to fill the ranks of the regular and reserve units. Unlike Allied divisions, they were quality and age related, providing attack, defensive, holding, Russian Front and line of communication divisions, with the best troops being siphoned off into the storm troop divisions. Unlike British divisions, many German divisions stayed on the same front for many months, in some cases years, affording them

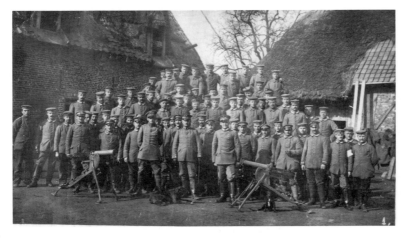

Officers and men of *I Machine Gun Company of III Battalion Grenadier Regiment 123 of 27 (Württemberg) Division* at rest somewhere behind the Sanctuary Wood positions.

A Belgian card showing the scale of the inundations near Ramscapelle. Two Belgian soldiers guard the narrow bridge.

an intimate knowledge of their combat zone. Each division had a history and often an ethnicity that could make it more reliable than another of the same age group and social background. Allied intelligence naturally kept a close eye on the make-up, history and combat-worthiness of each division, maintaining a full record on each on the Western Front.

The German Army was not a single entity. The Prussian Army, at eighty per cent of the personnel in the army, was the major component, but even in itself was not a single army. Serving in its ranks were troops drawn from the Grand Duchies of Baden, Hesse, Oldenburg, Mecklenburg-Schwerin, Mecklenburg-Strelitz and Saschen-Weimar, the Duchies of Anhalt, Saschen-Altenburg, Saschen-Coburg-Gotha and Saschen-Meiningen and the principalities of Lippe, Schaumburg-Lippe, Schwarzburg-Rudolstadt, Schwarzburg-Sonderhausen, Waldeck-Pyrmont and the two Reuss states. Also administered by the Prussian state were soldiers from the Imperial Lands of Elsass-Lothringen,

February in a Flanders trench. The soldier to the left of the sign is wearing the Württemberg cap cockade.

Concrete dug-outs in a quarry.

the state of Brunswick and the Hanseatic Free Cities of Bremen, Hamburg and Lübeck. The Kingdom of Bavaria was second in importance and fiercely independent.

A group of soldiers pose in a ruined house somewhere in Flanders.

Completing the German Army were the troops of two semi-independent states: Saxony and Württemberg. While Bavaria and Saxony had their own officer corps, in times of war all independent armies were subordinated to the Prussian Army that then controlled training, equipment and organisation. But this did not stop the rivalry between these states and Prussia. There are many recorded instances of departing troops, who had kept the sector quiet, sending messages to the enemy telling them the Prussians were coming and encouraging them to give them Hell.

An infantry division consisted of two infantry brigades, an artillery brigade and a cavalry regiment. As the troops came from specific areas, many of them had names as well as a number; *25 Infantry Division was* known as the *Hessian Grand Ducal Division,* while *40 Infantry Division* was alternately *4 Saxon Division.* In the same way many of the infantry regiments had two designations: regimental number in the army and then a territorial number; some had a further title that showed something about their history. Hence, *Infantry Regiment 169 was also 8.*

Many units had talented artists in their ranks. This Field Postcard was produced by a Corps printing unit from an original drawn by a soldier in its ranks. It shows the ruins of Hollebeke Château in late 1915.

Badisches Infanterie-Regiment from Baden, *Infantry Regiment 126* was known in Württemberg as *8. Württembergisches Infanterie-Regiment Nr.126 (Grossherzog Friedrich von Baden)* and *Infantry Regiment 36* was also *Füsilier-Regiment General-Feldmarschall Graf Blumenthal (Magdeburgisches) Nr. 36*.

The constitution stipulated that while the standing army should not exceed more than one per cent of the population, every male was liable for service over a twenty-seven year period from the close of his seventeenth to the forty-fifth year of his age. At the age of seventeen he was enrolled in the 1st Ban of the Landsturm, but was not called to active service until he was twenty. After two years with the colours, three years in the cavalry and artillery, and five and four years respectively with the reserve, at the age of twenty-seven he transferred to the 1st ban of the Landwehr for five years, to the 2nd Ban for seven years and finally at the age of thirty-nine he passed into the 2nd Ban of the Landsturm where he remained until his forty-fifth year. There was always an excess of recruits over the peacetime establishment, so nearly half of the potential intake was turned down for service and were simply added to the muster rolls of the 1st or 2nd Bans of the Landsturm or, if aged between twenty and thirty-two, were posted to the Ersatz Reserve.

This structure gave the German Army a large reserve of trained soldiers in time of war to add to its regular establishment of around 35,000 officers and over 650,000 NCOs and men: a reserve, an Ersatz Reserve, a Landwehr formed from trained soldiers and a Landsturm of untrained youths and middle-aged ex-soldiers. The latter were for duties inside the German frontiers but, as casualties mounted, many found themselves transferred to other types of formation. As a result of this, within a week of hostilities breaking out, nearly four million were serving with the colours, of whom over two million were deployed on the Eastern or Western Front.

With a population of over sixty-five million, the army was able to expand rapidly initially from ninety-two divisions at the start of the war to over 200 by the armistice. A brief history of those divisions that fought in Flanders is detailed below.

This record of divisions gives a clear indication of the speed of movement in the first few months of the war, and shows how quickly divisions moved from one front to another according to the needs of the advance or retreat. It also demonstrates that, as things settled down into trench warfare, divisions stayed in an area for long periods of time, some for most, if not the whole war, whereas, in the British Army, divisions moved along the front from army to army on a regular basis.

The Flanders front is often cited as being very active, but during certain periods it was much quieter than other parts of the front. While the battle of the Somme was taking place, the Flanders Front was a place to send divisions to rest and re-fit before going back. This record details both the transient and permanent divisions on the Flanders Front.

1915

1 and 2 Naval
Throughout the war the divisional staff of the two divisions stayed in place but the six regiments of the two divisions alternated between Zeeland and Schoorbakke, southeast of Nieuport. Both divisions stayed in Flanders for the whole war.

3 Bavarian
Remaining on the defensive for most of its service in Flanders, the division was used as a reinforcement in the Arras sector in June. After returning to Flanders it was sent to the Artois region in October and did not return until June 1917.

4 Bavarian
In April the division lost *8 Bavarian Reserve Infantry Regiment* to *10 Bavarian Division,* and in October the division left Flanders and was reassembled in the Artois region after detached units had fought at Loos.

A Train Column moving to a new area. The re-location of a division required hundreds of wagons to move the equipment, causing serious congestion during the preparations for an offensive.

A butcher's shop set up in a Brussels street.

4 Ersatz

The division stayed in the sector north of Dixmude for the whole of the year. At the end of July the battalions were grouped into regiments forming the *359, 360, 361* and *362 Regiments*. Along with *37 Landwehr Brigade* and *2 Reserve Ersatz Brigade,* it formed the *Werder Corps.*

4 Guards

Formed on the Russian front in March where it fought until being transferred to the Western Front on 10 October. After two rest periods and active service in the line, the division was moved to Flanders , where from 15 December it was involved in entrenching work in the Wytschaete-Messines sector.

5 Infantry

After considerable service in France and heavy losses in the Champagne attacks in September, the division was sent to Belgium in December where it was rested in the Hirson area.

6 Bavarian Reserve

The division remained in the Messines-Wytschaete sector until the beginning of March when it was relieved, with one regiment being sent to Neuve Chapelle and the others placed in rest before being sent to the Lille region.

10 Bavarian

Made up of recruits from Lower Bavaria and the Bavarian Palatinate, the division was formed in Belgium during March by taking infantry regiments from existing divisions. During April the division was stationed at Tournai and in May moved to the Somme.

26 Infantry

After fighting on the Eastern Front, *26 (Württemberg) Division* arrived and detrained at

A German position captured during a British attack near Zonnebeke.

Bertrix in Belgium on 20 November, moving to Courtrai in December where it re-joined *27 (Württemberg) Division,* to reform *XIII. Army Corps.*

30 Infantry

The division was attached to *Fourth Army* and was involved in the offensives to the south of Ypres. It lost *136 Regiment* to the newly formed *115 Division.*

38 Landwehr Brigade

In April, *38 Landwehr Brigade* took part in the second battle of Ypres in the Zonnebeke area. On 18 May it was transferred from Roulers to La Bassée to re-enforce *VII. Army Corps.* It was rested near Lille and went back into the line at the end of August in the Frelinghien-Houplines sector on the French/Belgian border in French Flanders.

Troops resting outside Ostend before moving to new positions.

39 Infantry

The division was involved in the Ypres offensives as part of *15 Corps* on the left wing of *Fourth Army*. In April, the division lost *171 Regiment* to *115 Division,* a new formation. During September *172 Regiment* suffered heavy losses; its eighth company alone received 111 men as replacements between 28 September and 16 October. The division remained in the vicinity of Ypres for the remainder of the year.

40 Infantry

Throughout the year, the division remained in the area between Ploegsteert and Grenier Wood. Some of its units were sent south as re-enforcements during the battles of Neuve Chapelle, Festubert and Artois. In March the division was reduced to three brigades, giving *133 Regiment* to *24 Division*.

43 Reserve

At the beginning of January, *86 Reserve Brigade* was in the line at Westende. Towards the end of February the division was reassembled and sent to rest in the vicinity of Menin-Roulers until 25 April. In May elements of the division were holding the sector Bixschoote-Boesinghe in the north of the salient. Another part of the division was sent as a re-enforcement to the Arras front to oppose the French offensive.

At the beginning of July, the division lost both of its brigades: *86 Reserve Brigade* to the offensive in Poland and *85 Reserve Brigade* to Lorraine.

44 Reserve

The division stayed in Flanders until 7 June when it was relieved from the Lombartzyde-Nieuport sector and transferred to the Eastern Front.

45 Reserve

The division remained in Flanders throughout the year. On 22 April it attacked in the Steenstraat sector and occupied the village of Lizerne temporarily. For the remainder of the year the division, like *46 Reserve,* held positions between Dixmude and Ypres without any important action, with periods of rest in the vicinity of Bruges and Thourout.

46 Reserve

Between 22 and 27 April the division was still holding the front north of Ypres and took part in the battles launched around Het-Sas, Lizerne and Steenstraat.

51 Reserve

The division remained in the area northeast of Ypres (Poelcapelle, Langemarck, St. Julien) for the entire year.

52 Reserve

The division remained on the front north of Ypres (Pilckem, St. Julien, Zonnebeke) throughout the year. During the fighting of April and May, *240 Reserve Infantry Regiment* had casualties of twenty five officers and 1,268 men.

53 Reserve

The division remained in line north of Ypres during the winter of 1914–15, alternating with *54 Reserve Division,* in the Broodseinde-Polygon Wood sector. It took part in the second battle of Ypres, near Frezenberg and Gravenstafel, where it lost heavily. After occupying the front between Wytschaete and St. Eloi during June, it returned to the northeast of Ypres to man the line at Verlorenhoek in the middle of July.

At the beginning of October the division lost *105 Reserve Brigade* as re-enforcements for the Champagne front. In November the division was regrouped and sent to rest north of Courtrai at Ingelmunster. It spent the winter behind the lines at Roulers.

54 Reserve

The division was around the Flanders front during the year: Becelaere, Polygon Wood, Menin Wood and the Roulers railway. It suffered heavy casualties during April and May when it fought at Frezenberg, Verlorenhoek and Hooge.

117 Infantry

The division was created by *Seventh Army* in the Ardennes in April; its three regiments came from *12 Division of VI. Corps* and *11 and 12 Reserve Divisions of VI. Reserve Corps.* The division arrived in Flanders via Champagne, Artois and Lens. After resting near Tourcoing, it took over the Messines sector at the end of October.

123 Infantry

The division was formed in April by taking three regiments from divisions of *XII and XII. (Saxon) Reserve Corps.* Moving from Champagne in May, the division went to the Artois

An observation balloon unit preparing a balloon for its ascent.

region where it fought at Loos. After a rest at Lille, the division went to Flanders in November where it held a sector south of the canal from Ypres to Comines.

1916

1 and 2 Naval

Involved in the siege of Antwerp in September 1914, it moved to guard the coast in November. The same month a second division was raised to assist *1 Naval*. Personnel for both divisions were Marines or Sailor Fusiliers recruited from the seamen or the general population of the port towns of Germany. Until reinforced with army recruits, they were classed as mediocre troops.

Throughout the war the two divisions remained in Flanders but three naval infantry regiments were detached and sent to the Somme at the end of September.

1 Guard Reserve

At the beginning of the war the division, forming, together with *3 Guard Division,* the *Guard Reserve Corps,* swept into Belgium as part of *2 Army.* At the end of September the division left for service on the Eastern Front. It returned to France to rest in late 1915, before being sent to Belgium at the start of 1916. During January and February it was employed on defensive works in the Wytschaete-Messines sector, while holding a sector in the region, as well as undergoing training in the Cambrai area. It then went to Artois and was committed to the Somme fighting at the end of July. After suffering heavy losses, the division was rested near Cambrai before being sent to a relatively calm sector north of Ypres, near the Ypres-Pilckem Road. It was sent back to the Somme.

British dead in a Flanders trench.

A large communal outdoor wash area.

3 Guard

After fighting at Namur in August 1914, the division was sent to Russia and then to France in April 1916. After fighting on the Somme with severe losses at Thiepval, in July, the division was sent to recover in the Dixmude area. In September it went to the Galicia Front and did not return to Flanders until late in 1917.

3 Reserve

Recruited in Pomerania, it formed part of *8 Army* under Hindenburg. After serving on the Eastern Front from the start of the war, the division was sent to Belgium to rest. It detrained at Bruges and remained in the district until 4 June when it was sent south to the Vendhuille-Bellicourt sector north of St. Quentin. A year later it returned to the Ypres sector.

Battalion horselines well behind the front line. Throughout the war, the German Army was more reliant on the horse than were the Allies, who had a greater production capacity for lorries and access to potentially unlimited amounts of fuel.

Landwehr officers and men in a rear position but close enough to the front for them to feel it neessary to have their gas masks with them.

4 Ersatz

The division was organised in August 1914 by grouping brigade ersatz battalions from Brandenburg Prussian-Saxony, Mecklenburg, Schleswig-Holstein and Hansa towns. After fighting in France, the division was sent to Belgium in late September 1914.

The division was kept in the region of Dixmude until April 1916 when part of it was sent east of Ypres between the Ypres-Roulers railway and the Comines canal, while the remainder of the division stayed in the line at Dixmude. Towards the end of September the division was sent to the Somme.

4 Guards

Formed on the Russian Front in March 1915, the division fought there until November when it was sent to the Arras Front. During December and February it built entrenchments in the region of Wytschaete-Messines and held the line at the same time.

It left the area for training and active operations with *1 Reserve Guards Division* at Arras and later on the Somme. The division returned for a week's rest in Flanders before holding a quiet sector north of Ypres from 17 September to 25 October, returning to the Somme on 6 November.

5 Ersatz

Organised in the autumn of 1915, the division was originally known as the *Basedow Division*. It comprised a Landwehr brigade from *26 Reserve Corps* and an ersatz brigade in the Dixmude sector. With *4 Ersatz Division*, it formed the *Werde Corps*. The division was in the line near the Yser and then southeast of Ypres between January and the end of September. It was sent to the Somme in October, minus a regiment that was lost to the newly formed *206 Division* in September.

11 Reserve

Recruited in Silesia, the division fought in Lorraine, at Verdun and then the Somme. After suffering enormous losses during the Somme battles, the division was sent to Flanders

The Kaiser often visited his troops on the Western Front. Here he is seeing life in the port of Zeebrugge.

A Flanders second line trench in the autumn – before the onset of the bad weather that would turn the baked clay into thick mud.

near the end of July where it was reconstituted with replacements from *12 Corps* depot. It was then rested and, at the beginning of August, sent to French Flanders, near Armentières.

At the end of September it returned to the Somme.

12 Reserve

The division fought in France from the beginning of the war in the Meuse-Argonne sector until early 1916. After serving at Verdun and on the Somme, the division was sent to Flanders from the beginning of August until the end of September. It occupied a sector south of Warneton. During this period it suffered heavy losses and was sent back to a quieter part of the Somme.

17 Reserve

Initially a coastal defence division in Schleswig-Holstein, the division was sent to Belgium on 23 August. By 9 September it had left for France.

After heavy losses on the Somme, the division was sent to Belgium at the beginning of

October. After a brief rest it was put in the line between Het Sas and the Ypres-Roulers railway from the end of October through to the end of January 1917.

18 Reserve
Released from guarding the coast in its native Schleswig-Holstein the division entrained for Belgium on 22 August. It advanced rapidly and after taking Louvain was involved in its sacking on 25 August. Two weeks later it was hastily transferred to the Oise area in France.

Heavy naval mortar in position in the dunes to shell approaching British ships.

    The division was withdrawn from the Somme to rest and re-fit after heavy losses and transferred to Belgium around the middle of October. By the end of the month the division was holding the line north of Ypres.

19 Landwehr
This division was formed in late 1916 with Landwehr regiments from Brandenburg, Westphalia and Saxony. Its battalions were Landsturm men from the Service of Supplies section of *Fourth Army*. At the beginning of October the division replaced *204 Division* in the Dixmude-Steenstraat sector where it remained for a year.

20 Landwehr
Formed at Roulers at the end of September with Landwehr Regiments from Prussian Saxony and Mecklenburg, its personnel were one-third returned wounded, and two-thirds from the supply services. At the beginning of October, the division replaced *206 Division* in the sector Dixmude-Schoorbakke, where it remained for over a year.

Like the army, the Marines had their own bands for parades and concerts.

24 (Saxon) Infantry

Recruited in the western part of the Kingdom of Saxony, the division formed part of *XIX Corps*. After fighting in Belgium it moved to Neuve Chapelle in March 1915. Having sustained very heavy losses on the Somme, it was withdrawn and transferred to Flanders about 11 November. It occupied the line between the Ypres-Comines Canal and the Douve river. Before coming to Flanders, it had had a good reputation, but it did not distinguish itself after its arrival there.

26 Infantry

A Württemburg division, it had fought in Belgium, Poland and Russia in 1914 and Serbia and Belgium in 1915. The division went into the line southeast of Ypres, between Hooge and the south of Sanctuary Wood, in January, after arriving in Belgium at the end of November. It held this sector until the end of July, suffering terrible losses on 2 July at Zillebeke.

After a period for recovery and re-inforcement, the division was sent to the Somme where it fought against the British at Longueval. It lost very heavily while resting at Guillemont between 18 and 19 August. On 25 August the division was relieved and sent back to Flanders, where it took over the Wytschaete sector between September and November. Around 11 November, the division left Flanders and returned to the Somme

27 Infantry

The division was raised in Württemberg and at the start of the war was part of *5 Army* in Lorraine. In December 1915 the division moved to Belgium and went into the line southeast of Ypres. Between January and July the division held the line between Sanctuary Wood and the Ypres-Comines Canal. On 24 February units of the division gained possession of the British trenches at Bluff, north of the canal, but lost them on 2 March. *123 Grenadier Regiment* lost very heavily in this action.

On 2 June, *26* and *27 Divisions (XIII. Royal Württemberg Corps)* made a violent attack on the Canadian positions in the Zillebeke sector, gaining possession of Observation Ridge, but being forced to abandon it as the result of a counterattack. The divisions lost heavily during the fighting.

The division was sent to the Somme at

The oldest soldiers belonged the Landsturm and were usually used to guard bridges and factories in occupied countries and in Germany. This Landsturmann is a member of *17 Battalion* of *III. Corps* recruiting district, sent to garrison Antwerp.

Marines looking after a future meal.

the end of July where it successfully resisted attacks against its positions but sustained serious losses. On 25 August it was relieved and returned to the Wytschaete sector where it remained until early November, when it was sent back to the Somme.

38 Division
At the outbreak of the war, the division, with *22 Division,* fought in the Belgian Ardennes as part of *XI Army Corps* in *3 Army.* It was moved to the Eastern Front in late August and the division did not return to the Western front until September 1915.

In 1916, after fighting at Verdun and then on the Somme, the division was sent in November to the Flanders coast between Ostend and the Dutch frontier to rest and reorganise. After a month of peace, the division was sent back to the Somme.

After a visit to Bruges, a marine from *1 Marine Infantry Regiment,* sent this card home.

Newly-arrived replacements celebrate their arrival in Flanders.

38 Landwehr Brigade

Created as an independent brigade, it fought in Belgium from 21 October 1914 until it was sent to the Arras front in March 1916. After six months' service in Artois it returned to French Flanders. It did not return to Belgium until 1918.

45 Reserve

Formed between August and October 1914, the division fought on the Yser in October where it suffered heavy losses; fifty-two officers and 1,699 men of *212 Reserve Infantry Regiment.*

Until 3 March 1916, the division occupied positions north of Ypres (Steenstraat-Boesinghe) with two of its infantry regiments that had temporarily been detached for service with *26 Infantry Division* in the Becelaere sector. The reformed division then took over the Messines sector and played no part in any important action until it was sent south to the Somme in September. It did not return to Flanders for a year.

46 Reserve

Formed in *9 Corps* district of the Hanseatic cities and Grand Duchy of Mecklenburg, it fought on the Yser and in Flanders during 1914 and 1915.

At the end of February, the division was relieved from its positions north of Ypres and transferred to Werwicq for two weeks before moving to the St. Eloi sector near Messines. The division suffered heavy losses at the beginning of April, being pulled out of the line to rest until May when it returned to the same sector. At the beginning of September, the division left for the Somme and did not return to Flanders.

54 Reserve

Composed mostly of recruits from Württemberg, its first action was at Ypres in October 1914. The division stayed in Flanders during 1915.

At the end of January, and the beginning of February 1916, the division was withdrawn

The main street
in Passchendaele
in 1916.

from the Ypres salient, and sent for training to the Beverloo Camp for two months, before being sent south to the Artois region. It returned to Flanders in October 1917.

58 Infantry
Although formed in Belgium during March 1915, the division went to the Artois front in May of the same year. After fighting in Russia in the latter part of the year, it returned to France where it was engaged in Lorraine, at Verdun, in the Champagne and on the Somme. After being heavily engaged in the latter battle, the division was sent to a calm sector on the Yser where it held the line from 19 September to 23 October. It then returned to the Somme during November. At the end of December it was again rested in Belgium before moving to the Verdun front.

117 Infantry
The division had taken over positions in the Messines sector at the end of October 1915 and remained in them until the beginning of March. For the next three months, the

Officers relaxing in their
quarters well behind the front.

An attempted salvage of a distressed observation balloon somewhere in Flanders.

division was first rested at Courtrai and then underwent a period of instruction and training at Beverloo Camp. At the beginning of June the division returned to the line, east of Ypres, near the road from Ypres to Menin. On 20 July the division was withdrawn and sent to the Somme.

123 Infantry

Formed in 1915, the division fought in France until mid-October when it was rested near Lille. Moving to Flanders in November, it held a sector south of the canal from Ypres to Comines. After resting near Bruges during the middle of March, it returned temporarily to the St. Eloi area around 9 April for front line service, before becoming the reserve division for the armies in the vicinity of Courtrai and Menin until 5 July. It was then sent to serve on the Somme and later in Russia. It did not return to Flanders.

185 Infantry

Initially only brigade strength when it was created in May 1915, it became a full division with the addition of *186* and *190 Regiments*. During 1915 it had served on the Somme, in Alsace and the Champagne before returning to the Somme in July 1916. After fighting on the Somme in July, the Aisne in August, and the Somme again in September and November, the division was sent to Alost in Belgium for a rest. A month later it was in the line to the south of Grenier Wood near Lille before returning to a sector north of Ypres in February 1917.

204 Infantry

Formed in Germany during June and July, its brigades came from Württemberg and Saxony. The *407 (413* and *414 Regiments)* and *408 (415* and *416 Regiments) Brigades*, after separate training, were brought together at the end of July and sent to Belgium. It was almost immediately put into the line near Dixmude and then southeast of Ypres.

At the end of the year, *415* and *416 Regiments* were taken from the front and given to *212 Division*. As a replacement, the division received *120 Reserve Infantry Regiment*

The soldiers of a telephone unit pose proudly with their field equipment.

(Württemberg) from *58 Division*. After further service at the front, the division moved to Alsace in June 1917.

206 Infantry

The division was organised in Belgium at the beginning of the year. It was composed of units from Brandenburg, Hannover and Schleswig-Holstein. After holding the Dixmude sector for a short while, the division was transferred to the Somme in October. It did not return to the Flanders front.

207 Infantry

Like *206 Infantry Division,* it was also formed in Belgium using brigades from Lorraine (*45 Reserve Division*), Pomerania (*46 Reserve Division*) and Schleswig-Holstein (*204 Infantry Division*). After formation in October, on the Belgian coast between Zeebrugge and Blankenberge, it went into the line in front of Ypres towards the end of November. It remained in the sector between the Zonnebeke-Ypres road and the Ypres-Comines Canal until the end of April 1917, when it went to the Artois.

211 Infantry

The division was organised on 15 September at Tournai with units from *27 Infantry, 17 Reserve* and *23 Reserve Divisions,* all of them having fought on the Somme prior to the transfer. After completing its organisation, the division was sent back to the Somme. It did not return to the Flanders front.

The shooting range near Poelcapelle.

Bibliography

Baer. C H. Der Völkerkrieg – Siebenter Band. Julius Hoffmann, 1916.

Baer. C H. Der Völkerkrieg – Zehnter Band. Julius Hoffmann, 1916.

Barton, P., Doyle, P., and Vandewalle, J. Beneath Flanders Fields: The Tunneller's War 1914-1918. The History Press Ltd., 2006.

Binding, R. A Fatalist at War. George Allen & Unwin, 1933.

Bull, S. German Assault troops of the First World War. Spellmount, 2007.

Chickering, R. Imperial Germany and the Great War, 1914-1918. Cambridge University Press, 2005.

Dewar, M. The First Flame Attacks. Volume 3 History of the First World War. Purnell, 1971.

Doyle, A.C. The British Campaign in France and Flanders 1916. Hodder and Stoughton, 1918.

Edmonds, Brigadier General Sir James, CB, CMG. Military Operations France & Belgium 1915, volume 1. Macmillan & Co, 1927.

Edmonds, Brigadier General Sir James, CB, CMG. Military Operations France & Belgium 1916, volume 1. Macmillan & Co, 1932.

Foley, R. German strategy and the path to Verdun. University Press Cambridge, 2005.

Görlitz, W(ed). The Kaiser and his court (the First World War diaries of Admiral Georg von Müller). Macdonald, 1961.

Gray, R & Argyle, C. Chronicle of the First World War Volume 1, 1914 – 1916. Facts on File, 1991.

Herwig, H. The First World War, Germany and Austria 1914-1918. Arnold, Headline Group, 1997.

Hölcher, G. Geschichte des Weltkriegs – Erster Band. Hoursch & Bechstedt, 1915.

http://www.greatwar.co.uk/ypres-salient/battles-ypres-salient.htm

Humphries, M O & Maker, J. (editors) Germany's Western Front: Translations from the German Official History of the Great War. Wilfrid Laurier University Press, 2010.

Junger. E. Storm of steel. Chatto & Windus, 1929.

Ludendorff, General. My War Memories 1914-1918 volume 1. Hutchinson (No Date).

Macdonald, L. The death of innocence. Headline, 1993.

Michelin & Cie. Ypres and the battles for Ypres 1914-1918. Michelin & Cie, 1920.

Nash, D.B. Imperial German Army Handbook. Ian Allan. 1980.

Ousby, I. The Road to Verdun. Jonathan Cape, 2002

Palmer, S & Wallis, S. A War in Words. Simon & Schuster, 2003.

Passingham, I. All the Kaiser's Men. Sutton Publishing, 2003.

Roynon, G. Massacre of The Innocents – The Crofton Diaries, Ypres 1914-15. Sutton Publishing, 2004.

Scheer, Admiral R. Germany's High Sea Fleet in the World War. Cassel & Co, 1920.

Schwink, O. Ypres, 1914 (The Battle on the Yser and of Ypres in the Autumn 1914). Constable, 1919.

Stone, D. Fighting for the Fatherland. Conway, 2006.

Sulzbach, H. With the German guns. Leo Cooper, 1973.

The Times. Documentary History of the War. Volume 8. The Times Publishing Company, 1919.

Thoumin, R. The First World War. Secker & Warburg, 1963.

Wegener, G. Der Wall von Eisen und Feuer – Ein Jahr an der Westfront. F A Brockhaus, 1915.

Westman, S. Surgeon with the Kaiser's Army. William Kimber, 1968.

Williams, J.F. Corporal Hitler and the Great War 1914 – 1918. Frank Cass, 2005.

Witkop, P (Ed.). German students' war letters. Pine Street Books, 2002.